Women in Gram Panchayats

Women in Gram Panchayats

Emerging Leaders in Grassroots Politics

S U N K A R I   S A T Y A M

PARTRIDGE

A Penguin Random House Company

To order additional copies of this book, contact
Partridge India
000 800 10062 62
orders.india@partridgepublishing.com

www.partridgepublishing.com/india

My Mother Sunkari Bhudevi Chinnaiah

Preface

The system of Panchayati Raj has always existed in different forms in India. The Panchayat system of the pre-British period was not statutory but voluntary. In this system, the village was the basic unit and every village had a council which consisted of the elderly people. The introduction of the Panchayati Raj to Indian polity was an attempt at the holistic development and democratization of the villages. During the first decade of an independent India, some laws were passed, and more recently, the constitutional directive has been interpreted as empowering the government to provide constitutional sanctions for important features, not only of village Panchayats but also of local self-governing bodies, particularly Gram Sabha. The democratic politics of India encourages only the elites to participate in elections, since only they possess the required education, knowledge, confidence, organizational and other skills, and material wealth. These are all needed for political participation. It is impossible, therefore, for poor people and for women to participate in democratic political processes and to have control over decisions which affect them. It is recognized that unless the poor and marginalized sections of society participate in the political process, the aims of democracy cannot be realized. Accordingly, it is necessary to bring the political system closer to them, and this demands democratic decentralization with enhanced popular participation.

At grassroots level, Panchayati Raj institutions are understood to play an important role in the welfare of marginalized sections of society and of women. So far, special representation has been given to them in Panchayati Raj institutions through the system of direct elections and nomination to local councils. The Seventy-third Constitutional Amendment Act has been hailed as a revolutionary step towards decentralization of power and governance. This amendment provides for the village assembly, the Grama Sabha, and also ensures uniformity in terms of tenure. Administrative units and all states are obliged to conduct periodic elections by an independent body. The introduction of the Seventy-third Constitutional Amendment Act in 1992 marks a new era in India's democratic system: it gives constitutional status to Panchayati Raj Institutions (PRIs) and strengthens them by ensuring regular elections (every 5 years); it reserves seats for Scheduled Castes, Scheduled Tribes and women (not less than one-third of seats); and provides various other institutional systems.

The present study aims to understand the nature and impact of women's leadership in the Panchayati Raj, with special reference to the villages of Srirampur and Chittapur in the Nizamabad district of Andhra Pradesh. The study examines whether women Sarpanches have made a real difference in these villages. Traditionally, leadership in the villages has been enjoyed by men who were, generally speaking, elderly and moderately educated, who belonged to the upper castes, who owned land and who had links with external authorities. It has been claimed that the Panchayati Raj in India would have resulted in the emergence of a new leadership in all parts of the country had the old and traditional rural elites been replaced. In this study we examine the hypothesis that the reforms of the Panchayati Raj system have brought about changes in the form and content of women's leadership at village level. The results of the study are also elaborated: economically sound and aged traditional village leaders were found to literally reject the concept of women's entry into grassroots politics. In contrast to this rejection by the rural elite, political parties are trying to gain membership among women and young people. However, women leaders desire to bring changes in the form of psychological and institutional transformation in village Panchayats.

This study's main objective is to understand the development of political consciousness, especially among Dalit women leaders; secondly, to clarify the challenges confronting women leaders within these two villages; and thirdly, to understand popular perceptions of the capabilities of women leaders. The study explores women's capabilities and performances in using resources effectively and lobbying for development projects. It also examines the degree of awareness of the members of Gram Panchayat about their powers and duties.

Since this study is intended to gather factual information in a systematic manner, it selected two villages, namely Srirampoor and Chittapoor Grama Panchayats, in the Balkonda Mandal and Nizamabad districts of Andhra Pradesh. The unit of study is only at Grama Panchayats, especially of elected ward members and sarpanches. Both qualitative and quantitative methods have been used for the collection of data. Regarding a sampling strategy, a survey was adopted covering forty elected members.

The present study is partly based on empirical research; it compares leadership qualities of male and female members at the level of Gram Panchayat in two villages namely Srirampoor and Chitapoor in Balkonda Mandal in the Nizamabad district of Andhra Pradesh. However, much attention was paid to Dalit women in order to interpret the issues concerning the study's objectives. It may be noted that the village of Srirampoor was newly created as a separate Gram Panchayat in 1996. Prior to that, it was small hamlet in Chittapoor. When it became an independent village, women were elected as Panchayat leaders, known as sarpanches. Previously, the village had only male sarpanches.

The data has been collected from two villages. Including village sarpanches and all Gram Panchayat ward members, forty respondents were interviewed. For this study, an intensive questionnaire and face-to-face interviews were used. This was useful in gaining proper information about the functioning of village sarpanches and about general political participation. Analysis of the general perceptions of sarpanches and ward members and selected villagers is presented. The data has been collected primarily from elected Gram Panchayat leaders such as ward members and sarpanches. As secondary sources, textbooks, articles, N.G.O reports, field research work, central and State government's occasional papers have been used. This study proves a useful attempt to show grassroots reflections on the functioning of Grama Panchayat in relation to women's leadership and their ability to overcome traditional socio-political challenges.

Acknowledgements

My sincere thanks to Prof. Kalpana Kannabiran, for her in-depth and deep rooted suggestions on how women in contemporary politics be understood from academic perspective. Her suggestions helped me to rethink and rewrite the manuscript effectively.

I express my sincere thanks to Prof. G. Sudharshanam (Department of Political Science, University of Hyderabad), Prof. I. Ramabrahmam (Department of Political Science, University of Hyderabad), Prof. P. Eashwaraih (Department of Political Science, University of Hyderabad), Prof. Chandrasekar Rao (Department of Political Science, University of Hyderabad), Dr. K.Y. Ratnam (Department of Political Science, University of Hyderabad) for their inspiration and suggestions, and Dr. L. Reddappa, Dr. Sujit Kumar Mishra, Dr. Sam Gundimeda, Dr. Soumya Vinayan and Dr. Sandhya Maliye (Council for Social Development) for their support.

I am extremely thankful to Dr. Vasanthi Srinivasan for her support and encouragement in completing present research study. Her guidance was extremely sound and helpful. My sincere thanks are also to Dr. R. Ramdas for his guidance and supervision in further researches.

My heart full thanks to Prof. P. Manikyamba for her support and encouragement throughout my University education.

My utmost thanks are due to my Manjula and sons Vivek and Vignan for their cooperation in academic research career and it is cordially appreciated. Without their support, it would not be possible to complete this text.

—Dr. Sunkari Satyam

Abbreviations

AP	Andhra Pradesh
BC	Backward Classes
CBO	Community Based Organisation
CDP	Community Development programme
DWACRA	Development of Women and Child in Rural Area
FGD	Focus Group Discussion
GOI	Government of India
GP	Gram Panchayat
GS	Grama Sabha
MLAs	Members of the Legislative Assembly
MPTCs	Mandal Parishad Territorial Constituency members
NCWA	National Convention of Women's Association
NES	National Extension Service
NGO	Non Governmental Organisations
PRIs	Panchayati Raj Institutions
SC	Scheduled Castes
SHG	Self Help Group
ST	Scheduled Tribes
VWC	Village Watershed Committee
WIA	Women's India Association"
ZP	Zilla Parishad (District Council)
ZPTCs	Zilla Parishad Territorial Constituency

Contents

Illustrations

List of Tables

Glossary

Grama Sabha - Assembly of people

Mandal - Cluster of villages (sub-district unit)

Mandal Panchayat Samiti - Block level Panchayati system

Sarpanch - Elected president through Panchayat election of the Village and Head of village panchayat

Ward – Sub-unit of the Gram panchayat

Zilla Parishad - District council under the PRIs

Chapter One

Women and Political Leadership

Research on the representation of women and their leadership has burgeoned in recent years, with considerable attention given to the links between the descriptive and the substantive. Many of these analysis focus on women's political performances as elected leaders, the constraints and opportunities they face in seeking to advance 'woman-friendly' positions. Yet recent studies have reached an understanding that women's place in politics has become 'narrow in quantity' and 'abnormal in political opportunity'. The fact is that any change in society takes time, and building a women political career and her capacity to influence political participation require the government to initiate more policies. But whether policies do, in fact, meet the essential social requirements to encourage women into politics is the fundamental question in this context. Generally, political leadership is influenced by factors such as individual, structural and politico-cultural constraints and/or the expansion of opportunities for women politicians to enter government, where there is arguably considerable potential for them to act. In studying women's political leadership in contemporary political settings, it is essential to look at case study research which concentrates on individual women, highlighting the unique characteristics that led them to assume a political career.

The literature and documentation concerning women leaders at national, provincial and state levels show long-standing serious debate in academic, development and policy circles. Women of mainstream societal or political backgrounds have been highly focused upon, and rigorous research has been made of their achievements and outstanding contributions. But there have been few opportunities for academic research on issues of existing and emerging Dalit women's leadership in grassroots politics, taking into account their societal constraints and political marginalisation as well as their limited or constrained political choices, though there has been more focus on these issues recently. It is clear that studies were conducted on women in the Panchayati Raj but not on the deep-rooted socio-political issues of Dalits in general and women of Dalit background specifically. With the gaps in knowledge so widespread and the issue so deep-rooted, this study is a modest attempt to fill the gaps and provide a discussion on grassroots leadership of Dalit women in the context of Panchjayati Raj Institutions (PRIs).

In India, affirmative action for women and disadvantaged groups has been enshrined in the Constitution through the promotion of PRIs. The Constitutional 73rd Amendment Act of 1992 reserved a minimum of one-third of seats for women (both as members and as chairpersons). More recently, in 2009, the government of India approved the reservation of fifty percent of seats in PRIs for women, and many states, including Rajasthan and Odisha, have passed similar legislation. According to Article 243(B) of the Constitution of India, Grama Sabha is a "body consisting of persons registered on the electoral rolls relating to a village within the area of Panchayat, at the village level." The Panchayati Raj (Rule of Village Committee) system is a three-tier system in the state with elected bodies at Village, Taluk (Block) and District levels. It ensures greater participation of people and more effective implementation of development programmes in rural areas (ICRW – UN Women Joint Publication, NA:1).

The present chapter will initially elaborate on the available literature on the leadership, and to some extent women's political rights movements in India, to substantiate the present focus of study. The study was initially about women's leadership of PRIs, especially at the grassroots level popularly known as Grama Panchayats, with special reference to the villages of Srirampur and Chittapur in the Nizamabad district of Andhra Pradesh.

This study examines how women from Dalit communities have entered into grassroots politics, by what channels and how they are elected into representative governance, and whether women sarpanches have made a real difference in selected villages. Traditionally, leadership of villages has been enjoyed by men who, generally speaking, were moderately educated elders belonging to the upper castes, who owned land and had links with external authorities. It has been claimed that the Panchayati Raj system in India would have resulted in the emergence of a new leadership in all parts of the country had the old and traditional rural elites been replaced. In this study we examine the hypothesis that reforms of the Panchayati Raj system have brought changes to the form and content of women leadership at the village level.

Normally, only women who have their husbands or families' political support and close and direct connections with powerful authorities like politicians and district level leaders become village leaders. Irrespective of caste or class, women leaders generally face discrimination from society in the form of bitter words regarding their capabilities locally. The view that women's capabilities are undermined by marriage and familial and social relations was aptly substantiated by Kannabiran, Kalpana et al (2004). As a result, women tend to withdraw from public life because, whenever they wanted to bring about real change, they faced regular threats of violence in the form of gender and caste discrimination. And yet, rural women are bravely asserting themselves in different regional contexts in India.

This study aims to understand the development of political awareness in two villages. Following the Seventy-third Amendment, people (*marginalised sections – Scheduled Castes (SC), Scheduled Tribes (ST) and BC*) in general and women in particular have gained an institutional space to participate in local politics and decision-making processes. This is evident in the present literature on PRIs to some extent: rural people have expressed their urgent needs and have debated on how to address them through the system of the Panchayati Raj. This study analyses popular perceptions of women in leadership. More specifically, it attempts to highlight women's views on the politics of Grama Panchayat. Before focusing on PRIs and their leadership, the following questions are addressed: What is leadership? Are there any developments on women's rights and their place in the political arena? How are women being supported to emerge as leaders and to improve their leadership qualities?

Women in Leadership Paradigm

Leadership is a strong and important element in any society, leading it into social prosperity. "Leadership is an essential feature of all government and governance: weak leadership contributes to government failures, and strong leadership is indispensible if the government is to succeed. Wide leadership secures prosperity in the long run; foolhardy leadership may bring about a catastrophe. The lack of leadership routinizes governance" (Masciulli. J et al, 2009:3). Such an important element of politics and state affairs, the word 'leadership' can be traced back ancient Egypt (Karin Klenke, 1996). As a word, leadership is derived from the verb 'to act' in early Greek and Latin. Two Greek verbs, *archein* (to begin to lead, to rule) and *prattein* (to pass through, to achieve) correspond to the Latin verb *agere* (to set into motion, to lead). (Jennings 1960, *quoted by Karin Klenke 1996*). *The Concise Oxford English Dictionary* defines a 'leader' as 'the person who leads or commands a group, organisation, or country'. Leadership is a group process through which individuals initiate

3

activities to achieve the common objectives of the group or community by working together, stimulating each other, supplementing abilities and resources and evolving on an effective organizational structure. Leadership is a crucial element in making people participates in the process of change. The visions and perceptions of leaders play powerful roles in engaging the populace. Leadership is quite indispensable in influencing people to cooperate towards a common goal and to create situations to enable collective responses. Commenting on the role of leadership, Iltiza Khan states that "leadership is thus the *sine qua non* of success in all human activities, but in a democratic system, particularly at the lower levels, it assumes greater significance and wider proportions" (Desai Vasant, 1979).

Pigor says that leadership is a process of mutual stimulation by which an individual can resolve relevant differences and human energy can be controlled in pursuit of a common cause. Leadership is also an effective instrument of interest identification, interest articulation and interest aggregation (Bhargava, B.S, 1990).

Formal leadership in a village is enjoyed by those who hold any official position such as membership of the Panchayat bodies; but villagers attach greater importance to informal leaders than to formal leaders. A man who is called upon to settle disputes or to discuss village problems is regarded as an informal leader whether or not he enjoys any official position. He achieves this position by becoming a 'Headman' (Inamdar, N.R 1970). He achieves a commanding influence over others because of his financially sound position, his ability to advance loans to the needy and to provide jobs for people, and his appearing wise and fair. His followers accept him because they have confidence in his abilities. The necessary characteristics of an informal leader are that he should have a caste standing, a good economic position, and be advanced in age. He should not be in the race or struggle for power. No informal leaders are practically active.

Leadership as a concept deals with personal character and the individual's ability to make his/her supporters follow as he/she wishes to bring about change. Political leaders affect outcomes and attain or fail to attain good or evil group ends, through their attempts to intelligently use soft and hard power innovatively and adaptively in particular and general situations and contexts (Nye 2008; Heifetz 2007; Kellerman 2004 quoted by Masciulli. J et al 2009).

Leaders in all situations and contexts need to communicate a culturally resonant vision beyond their merely self-interested career goals. Political leadership, the art of initiating collective agency and directing oneself and one's followers, overlaps significantly with higher levels of military, judicial, organizational, religious and ideological leadership. Political leadership is a part of social leadership in general, but its boundaries are difficult to delimit because of the cultural and regime contexts in which it is contextualized. Leaders have ethical and power profiles that are always embedded in political culture and institutions. Leadership includes symbolic activity mediated by culture, since leaders, as 'identity entrepreneurs', are engaged in providing myths and visions to create, reshape or enhance national and other political cultures in a general process of innovative adaptation to environmental challenges (Wildavasky 2006, quoted by Masciulli J. et al 2009).

In a democracy, power is legitimated through popular electoral mandates, and leadership is based on the popular will. In the context of democracy in India, such a mandate has been continuously enshrining and new factors like caste and social mobility have emerged as very important. In political terms, periodic elections and rule of law are in and of themselves proving much better instruments to change reality for citizens, especially with respect to gender inclusivity. In the current system, people serve the political leadership. Servant leadership has emerged through Panchayati Raj Institutions to empower the common man and woman to control their leaders and attain true emancipatory politics.

Political leadership, specifically, is part of a game of power, electoral politics and great followership, but in general contexts, political leadership is closely related to social beliefs, values, cultural characteristics, ethical values, attitudes and actions of leaders and followers, as well as their historical situation and cultural-institutional context (Nye, 2008). As pointed out by Masciulli J. et al (2009), leadership is a symbolic activity mediated by culture, for leaders as 'identity entrepreneurs' are engaged in providing myths and visions to create, reshape or enhance national and other political cultures.

In the process, leaders and followers themselves are affected by what they help create (Rousseau 1987, The Social Contract II, 7, quoted by Masciulli J. et al, 2009). Political leadership implies followership as well as group tasks to be accomplished through innovative adoption in a specific situation and institutional-cultural context (Heifetz 1994; Tucker 1995; Nye 1999; Bennis and Thomas 2002; Nye 2008, quoted by Masciulli J. et al 2009).

Based on the existing literature reviewed by Masciulli J. et al (2009), the following elements in defining political leadership can be identified: "the personality and traits of leaders or leaders, including her or his ethical and cultural character; the traits and ethical-cultural character of the followers with whom the leader interacts (keeping in mind that leaders of different followers and followers of different leaders interact as well, cooperatively or competitively); the societal or organizational context in which the leader-follower interaction occurs – general culture, political culture, political climate, norms, and institutions; the agenda of collective problems or tasks which confront the leaders and followers in particular historical situations; the nature of the leader's interpretive judgment, since situations do not define themselves, but have to be defined by leaders' insights accepted by the followers; the means – material and intangible – that the leaders use to attain ends and/or their followers' goals; these are 'the techniques which the leader uses to mobilize support on behalf of her or his agenda and/or to maintain support or position (Peele, 2005: 192, quoted by Masciulli J. et al, 2009:5).

Women's Movements for Political Rights

Since, to some extent, thorough studies have attempted to understand leadership, political leadership and women's leadership and its elements, it is essential also to present historical issues concerning women's struggles and their political rights movements. There have been struggles, advocacies and campaigns throughout the world for equal rights for women, especially in Western countries, since the eighteenth century. The demands by concerned activists and women's groups have gradually expanded from social to political (Jyotirmay, M. 2003). Continuous expansion of self-awareness, respect and dignity through various social and political movements, using methods like advocacy, campaigns and political and social mobilizations, led to various institutional measures by nations.

Here I have tried to trace historical evidence of struggles and movements for equal rights, equal status and political leadership. However, since the present research was focused on women leadership primarily, it would be appropriate to look at the literature in this area. With regard to women leaders, the first of these were found in the pantheons of many ancient cults as mother goddesses, female deities and priestesses of either male or female gods (Karin Klenke, 1996). In the context of politics and religion, the appearance of women leaders dates back to the mid-1800s. The women's movement for political right (suffrage) was spearheaded by a number of passionate and influential women (Paxton, P. & Melanie M. Hughes 2007:34).

According to Klenke, based on her review of the literature, women began to emerge as leaders in social movements in large numbers in the nineteenth century. Especially after the Civil War, America saw the beginnings of a massive effort to win rights for women in politics and other social spheres. In the twentieth century, women's movements in the West began to highlight inequality in the political sphere. In the initial stages, the women's movement concentrated on equal opportunity in political, economical and social spheres. In this period, women's organizations were formed to achieve equal status in the political, administrative and judicial processes. Through these organizations and their efforts, women leaders emerged and initiated movements, and state policies had began to rectify gender bias in lawmaking and enforcement, and in overall political culture.

Emergence of Women's Rights Based Campaign

In the forefront of the history of women in politics, New Zealand was the first country to grant women the right to vote in 1893. This move was inspired by the equal-rights arguments of the philosopher John Stuart Mill. In fact, he strongly advocated adult franchise and women's rights. The success of New Zealand's initiation of women's political rights led to further widespread movements, especially in the United States of America, Canada and other western countries. In the USA, the women's movement for political rights began with the National Women's Suffrage Association (NWSA), headed by Elizabeth Candy Stanton and Susan B. Anthony. As a result of the movement for political rights under leadership of NWSA, the US government brought a bill: the passage of the Nineteenth Amendment. It is important to note that the women's bill was named the Anthony Amendment, through which the right to vote was granted on August 18th 1920 (Paxton, P. & Melanie M. Hughes 2007:47). Prior to the US's move on women's rights, other countries had already granted suffrage to women: Austria in 1902; Finland in 1906; Norway in 1913; Denmark and Iceland in 1915; Canada in 1917; Austria, Estonia, Georgia, Germany, Ireland, Kyrgyzstan, Latvia, Poland, Russia and the United Kingdom in 1918; Belgium, Belarus, Kenya, Luxemburg, the Netherlands, Sweden and Ukraine in 1919; Albania, the Czech Republic, Slovakia and the USA in 1920. Gradually, other nations have granted franchise rights and political spaces, and very recently Kuwait also gave political rights to women in 2005 (Paxton, P. & Melanie M. Hughes 2007:47-49).

A significant landmark in the history of women's movements for self-respect and political identity was the declaring of 1975 as International Women's Year by the United Nations (UN) General Assembly, which gave a further boost to women's political empowerment. Consequently, and importantly, all over the world, 18.75 percent of seats in national assemblies were allotted to women, and women made up one-quarter of all elected deputies in the People's Council of Bulgaria (Jyotirmay, M. 2003). As such, Hungary, Germany, Poland, Romania, Mongolia, Vietnam, India, Bangladesh and Pakistan gave significant political positions to women.

The Indian Context

Women's movements in pre-independence India influenced the elite group of Hindu and Muslim men and women, because from the beginning the Indian women's movement was oriented towards elite representation and not towards mass mobilization. The caste disparity which the Hindu religion sanctions and strengthens did not allow the elite women of India to consider the problems of low caste women (Mandal, J. 2003:226). Women's movements were actually emerged from the upper caste male dominant personalities, and they highlighted women's problems as whole but not differentiated based on caste.

Initially, the Indian women's movement was begun by Raja Ram Mohan Roy (1772-1833), from a social reform point of view which focused on sati and kulin polygamy and which supported women's property rights. Following the same line of thought, Ishwarchandra Vidyasagar campaigned for widows to be allowed to remarry. In both these cases, women were facing social issues like inequality, inferior status, enforced seclusion, lack of education and early marriage. Further, women-based social reform movements were started by others committed to social reformation.

Social reformers like Keshub Chandra Sen, a prominent Brahmo Samaj leader, had started a women's journal and developed educational programmes for women. Other reformers like Narayan Ganesh Chandavarkar, Madhav Govind Ranade and R.G. Bhandarkar and Mahipatram Rupram Nilkanth worked for equal status for women in different parts of the country. Some women's associations had begun to work for the cause, taking the lead from western efforts. By the end of the nineteenth century, a few socially aware women emerged and worked to bring women into mainstream society. Among those were Swarnakumari Devi and Ramabai Saraswati. The third session of the Indian National Congress's Conference (1887) provided a women's platform and a more specific section, named Bharat Mahila Parishad, was formed in 1905 to discuss social issues like child marriage, the status of widows and other socially evil customs.

In the twentieth century, the contribution of Gandhi to the emancipation of women is also worth noting. In 1917, the Women's India Association (WIA) was established by Annie Beasant and Margaret Cousins to mobilize women toward self-development. The Women's India Association worked to bring Indian women into the mainstream of Indian politics. In 1924, the National Convention of Women's Associations, held at Allahabad, adopted a resolution for equality of rights between men and women to be incorporated into the constitution (Sudhir Verma 1997). Another women's organization, The All India Women's Conference, came into existence in 1929, mainly campaigning for social reforms, such as the Sarada Bill, and for women's franchise. During the 1920s and 1930s, tremendous changes occurred in the women's movement in India.

In the first round table conference in 1930-31, two Indian women – one Hindu and one Muslim, chosen by the British government as India's official representatives, supported the Simon Commission's recommendation that 2.5% of seats be reserved for women; but they did not agree with the proposal to reserve seats on communal lines. At the Karachi session of Congress in 1931 under the leadership of Sarojini Naidu, all of the women's organizations were unanimous in the decision that women should enter into the legislature on equal terms with men without any favours in the shape of reservation, nominations or co-option of seats. They also rejected any wifehood qualifications.

Gandhi was also against reserved seats and demanded total equality for women. At the second round table conference in 1937, Begum Shanawab, one of the official women representatives, was sympathetic to reservation of seats for women on communal lines. The other official representative, Mrs. Radha Bai Subbarayan, in spite of Mahatma Gandhi's efforts to convince her, insisted that without reservation of seats women would find it difficult to contest (Sudhir Verma, 1997). Both strongly supported reservation of seats for women but a stratified reservation based on caste was never permitted to be discussed until the recent debate about caste-based reservation for women.

Women in Leadership – Stimulating Factors in India

In the present political context, the issue of women in leadership positions is highly focused upon by research scholars. Women in politics as an issue of social change, with the UN's dedication of the year of 1975 to women and the subsequent World Decade for Women, have prompted governments to devise special policy measures and to initiate constitutional reforms to improve women's situation. Any leadership is actually an outcome of participation in political and social movements, in campaigns and in matters of advocacy.

India is predominantly a patriarchal society in which a system of male-led dominance prevails, but also there is strong caste system in which hierarchically upper castes dominate and enjoy social supremacy. But the current form of democracy is largely a liberal one (rule by the few), usurping real democracy (rule of the majority) via popular elections. In this society, castes interact to promote exploitation of one by the other along multiple axes: of the poor by the rich, of the people of lower classes (castes) by higher economic classes. The lines of exploitation are not as precise as suggested here, but they roughly follow the contours of casteism. Any discussion of political leadership that wishes to understand the marginality of women in politics must begin by acknowledging these intersections.

The subject of women in leadership is no exception from the above matters. But how many women are allowed to participate in such public spheres within these socio-cultural constraints? The majority of studies reveal evidence of low participation of women in political and social systems. As Joshi, A.H. (2010) points out "even in egalitarian, democratic and industrially developed societies, women political leaders have not come to the fore. Though the nature of politics, the types of political systems or ideologies and the structures of political institutions are contributing factors in determining the degree of women's participation, the socio-cultural and historical conditions appear to have stronger influence. Politics too is socially, culturally and historically bound (2010:8)."

Active leaders in the specific context of rural areas, on the other hand, are leaders in the sense that they have power over the fortunes of others and that they organize village affairs. Their chief mark of identification is that they are men who can get things done their way despite the challenges from other, less powerful people. They are recognized as persons of power. In earlier times, before the introduction of the Panchayati Raj system, the village leaders came from the dominant caste groups. They were propertied men of the village, had a high caste status and had some education compared to the common villagers, who were mostly uneducated. Their power was legitimized by the traditional social structure.

Though there is a strong traditional social system dominating the political arena, some stimulating factors, especially those such as the Seventy-third Amendment Act, the Women's Reservation Bill and the Self Help Groups (SHGs) movement contributed to women entering politics. According to a report of the Inter-Parliamentary Union (1999) on the participation of women in political life, an assessment of the developments in national parliaments, political parties, governments and the Inter-Parliamentary Union has brought to light some important contributing factors in women's political participation. The major factors are: the state's observable willingness to encourage the greater participation of women, an attitude that has been enhanced and encouraged by its policies; the political parties' intention to increase women's participation in their party affairs; internal leadership structures; raised awareness of the importance of women voting; all parties' claims to analyze voting results with a view to assessing the respective chances of success of men and women; the intentions expressed by the party leadership or "recommendations" by party leaders to the grassroots; the strengthening of local bodies and Acts and Amendments; the stipulated representation of women in leading political party bodies; the adoption of a quota system; the adoption of a system for alternating women's and men's names on lists; the requirement that women be placed in positions of eligibility on voting lists; measures to ensure the fair distribution of women and men in constituencies in which the party was most likely to win seats; logistic and financial backing, etc (Inter-Parliamentary Union, 1999).

Along with national and international covenants, PRIs came into existence to encourage broad-based popular participation, but women's participation has lagged behind. In rural India, women had no opportunity to enter into politics because of patriarchal biases. Women's marginality in politics, political leaderships' continued exclusion and decision-making terrains are products of the history of patriarchal legacies in India. This is true of both the colonial and post-independence states.

But in recent times, women have been engaging with men in all sectors including politics, administration and business. For example, in Andhra Pradesh, the Development of Women and Child in Rural Area (henceforth DWACRA) and Self Help Group (SHGs)) members are playing an important role in rural politics as informal leaders. These groups have also emerged as interest groups demanding their own community benefits. In India, with its complex and rigid social, political and cultural settings, most women entering into politics or exercising their power do so by virtue of personal influence. Personal determination and dedication to political progress is still a matter of familial connections. Formal leadership, in my opinion, varies by caste, class, culture and religion, but women's leadership qualities still depend on family as well as on these structures. In these circumstances, an attempt to understand the leadership of Dalit women at the grassroots level must ask the basic research question of how their leadership qualities are assessed. What are the determining factors allowing them to emerge as leaders? How are they treated by specific societies in specific social systems? These research questions were asked regarding women's leadership in PRIs, with special reference to the district of Nizamabad of Andhra Pradesh State.

Chapter Two

Review on Women in Grassroots Politics

The Panchayat Raj Institutions, as a small wing of the self-government system, are the institutions of local elected governments including both urban and rural areas. They are institutionally constituted through the Seventy-third Amendment Act by the government of India. As discussed in the previous chapter, the grassroot level institutions of the Panchayat Raj are divided into three tiers: the village Panchayats, the middle level intermediary Panchayats and the district level Zilla Panchayats. Against this background, for the last twenty years many Indian thinkers, activists, observers and researchers have contributed to the development of ideas regarding the Panchayat Raj system, particularly from the mid 1990s onwards. In the modern democratic process in India, the most forceful rights of village people came through these local governance institutions, and policy level outcomes and societal and political changes in the system were recorded by social scientists, academics and policy makers. In this chapter, I review some of the extant literature in order to clarify the relevance of my study. The existing literature is classified into three categories based on the following areas of specific research: i. General studies highlighting problems and prospects; ii. Specific studies on Andhra Pradesh; and iii. Studies on women's participation and leadership in Panchayat Raj Institutions.

General Studies on the Panchayati Raj

Initially, I have tried to cover the reviews on the national system towards a broad understanding of the scenario and the current issues, so that this study will be more in-depth with specific context. Among the broad review sources, the study by Ruth J. Alsop, Anirudh Krishna and Disa Sjoblom on 'Inclusion and Local Elected Governments: The Panchayat Raj System in India' showed the functional aspects of the Panchayat Raj system in the states of Madhya Pradesh and Rajasthan. This study focuses extensively on fifty-three villages using two integrated methodologies: a structured questionnaire and an intensive anthropological investigation. The study aims to assess the degree and nature of exclusion and inclusion within Panchayat Raj organizations in these two states.

The study has drawn some important findings from grassroots observations. It observed that participation in the election of Panchayats is high, but that high voter turnout was not indicative of an overwhelming interest in the process of democracy of local government. The influential factors of decision making in the election are found to be: social solidarity; avoidance of tension within the village; bribery; fear of exclusion and poverty; and often simply the thrill of participating in the festivities of elections. Regarding the choice of candidate to vote for, the villagers take into account both personal attributes like education, trustworthiness, age and gender if female, and broader considerations such as the candidate's household's overall economic and social position, the strength of economic relations between the candidate's household and the voter's household, and bribes paid. There is an obvious and disturbing indication that villagers are at present more concerned with consolidating existing economic and social relations than using the democratic process to change inequitable rural societies (Ruth J. Alsop et al, 1999). Further, it is observed that social and economic factors are still the predominant factors influencing grassroots politics, but focus on such traditional social issues may derail the objective of these democratic decentralised institutions.

Vasant Desai, in his study, focuses on rural self-government processes. He advises that power should be in the hands of the people. The primary objective of the Panchayat Raj is to strengthen democracy at grassroots level on the one hand, and increase powers as well as responsibilities of the people on the other, so as to allow them to manage their affairs in the best possible manner. He observed that recent developments in Panchayat Raj Institutions have facilitated the strengthening of the democratic process and self- rule institutions in rural areas (Vasant Desai, 1979).

Further, many research studies have highlighted the importance of the Panchayat Raj Institution (PRI). For example, Harichandran's work focuses on rural people's perceptions. The major objective of the study is to ascertain the awareness among various groups of the concept and workings of Panchayat Raj system. He finds that the concept of Panchayat Raj is well known to rural people and that the active participation of government officials and elected members has enhanced general interest in Gram Panchayat politics in recent years (Harichandran, C. 1998).

Prof. Hoshiar Singh exposes some of the glaring lacunas in the Panchayat Raj system. He discusses the features of the Seventy-third Constitutional Amendment Act, its strength and weaknesses and whether it strengthened the Panchayat Raj system in this country. The concept of Panchayat Raj itself has undergone changes. It has expanded to cover areas of rural development and economic planning. However, there is no clarity about the relationship between Panchayat bodies and development programmers. However, there is talk of decentralizing powers to lower level bodies, while continuing with the centralized power system. Moreover, the Seventy-third Amendment Act attempted to provide meaningful decentralized bodies in the country by insisting on regular elections on expiry of their term, making them financially viable, involving them in micro-level planning etc. But the act has little to offer to the Panchayats in terms of functions, powers and resources to shape them as units of local self-government (Hoshiar Singh, 1993). In addition, he says that the task was left to each state to legislate according to local needs, but the existing federal structures of polity are yet to be supported functionally. This is particularly true with regard to states' powers to exercise and implement the Act of the Seventy-third Amendment, transferring local issues such as regular elections of Gram Panchayats, allocation of funds and strengthening of Grama Sabhas to grassroots institutions.

Despite the loopholes, he says, the act is certainly a step forward in facilitating the power of decision-making in rural communities. This sort of democracy at grassroots level creates responsive village Panchayats. It targets the system of Gram Panchayat to improve conditions for people through periodic village assemblies, regular elections, sufficient representations of the weaker sections of society like SCs, STs and women (Hoshiar Singh, 1993). If the provisions of the Act are implemented sincerely, they are capable of strengthening Panchayat Raj bodies in the country.

O.P. Bohra, in his study, on 'Women in Decentralized Democracy' focused primarily on the Seventy-third Amendment Act and its goal of popular participation in decentralized democratic institutions. He argued that the decentralization of power means that it has to provide social justice, gender equality and the empowerment of socially marginalized sections of society as well as of women. Moreover, a decentralized democratic process needs to provide a platform for, and give a voice to, socially marginalized sections and women in grassroots institutions and public spaces like Grama Sabha, and other meetings in which their feelings of solidarity will be understood in a justified manner in a wider social and political context. Bohra further says that affirmative action has to build a critical mass of local leadership of these groups and that they should participate actively in the strategic decision-making of PRIs.

Krishna Chakraborthy and Swapan Kumar Bhattacharya's study conducted in Nabagram, a medium-sized multi-caste village in the district of Hooghly in West Bengal, analyses whether the present (post-1978) system of Panchayati Raj in West Bengal has brought about qualitative changes in the traditional arrangement of distribution of power (Krishna Chakrabottty 1993). In their opinion, the introduction of PRIs and universal adult suffrage has notably changed the traditional base of power its mode of operation in rural areas. However, they conclude that substantial fundamental and qualitative changes have not taken place as was intended. They observe that factional disputes continue to dominate village politics.

Some committees have expressed the need to restrict the hold of political parties in PRIs (Bhargava, B.S. 1990). However, it is significant to note that none of these committees suggested a ban of political parties on the statute books. On the contrary, the Santhanam committee explicitly recommended that there should be no legal provision prohibiting political parties from influencing Panchayati Raj elections. These committees suggested that political parties should be prevented from nominating candidates for Panchayats and from allotting party symbols to various candidates in the Panchayat elections. The Siddiq Ali and Santhanam committees recommended that political parties should not be recognized for the purpose of Panchayat elections. Preventing political parties from participating in elections and in the operation of Panchayati Raj bodies, requiring election results to be unanimous, promoting consensus in the working of Panchayati Raj institutions and making Panchayats politics-free zones have all been suggested in various studies.

In contrast, B.S. Bhargava carried out empirical work on the role of political parties in the Panchayati Raj. He opined that the successful functioning of Panchayati Raj system depends to a great extent on the role of political parties and the nature of politics generated within the system. He pointed out that the Panchayati Raj system has brought rural leadership into the mainstream of national politics. In his observations, political education and the political socialization of rural people are the natural consequences of the process.

A recent study on "A Silent 'Revolution'? Women's Empowerment in Rural Tamil Nadu", by Staffan Lindberg, Venkatesh B Athreya, R Vidyasagar and Göran Djurfeldt, raised some important issues relating to social changes resulting from women's entry into local politics at village level Panchayats via the thirty-three percent reservation system, according to the Constitutional (Seventy-third Amendment) Act 1992, and their membership of self-help groups to access micro-credit to met their financial requirements. The report includes a twenty-five year panel study of 213 agrarian households in six villages in the Karur and Tiruchirapalli districts of the state of Tamil Nadu. The study observes that there is some evidences of the increased participation of women in the non-agricultural labour market. Based on interviews with selected female respondents, it is observed that there was "collaboration between husband and wife in running the Panchayat when a women president or vice president is in a complex situation, such as arranging a contract for construction work to be undertaken for the Panchayat, conducting board meetings jointly and sharing responsibilities when dealing with the people of village" (Staffan Lindberg et al. 2011).

This study included case studies to find out the reasons and the challenges of women in grassroots politics. It yielded some important findings: that women leaders have the support of their husbands; that they support their husbands' relationships with the people and their association with political parties at election time; and that they encourage active involvement in the affairs of Grama Panchayat. Thus the report in some way concluded that "on the basis of empirical findings, the reservation for women in grassroots politics has not only changed the conditions for local collective action, but has led to several potentially positive advances for women as well as for the local political system and administration" (Staffan Lindberg et al. 2011).

Thus the report raises some important issues regarding to women entering politics: constitutional provision has helped women to enter into real politics and to play an active role, and they enjoy support from family members, especially their husbands. Another issue is the formation of self-help groups which offer financial support and provide self-employment opportunities.

Ruth J. Alsop, Anirudh Krishna and Disa Sjoblom's study focuses primarily on the nature of exclusion and inclusion within the system of Panchayat Raj in the states of Rajasthan and Madhya Pradesh. The selected districts in the present study are Ajmer, Bhilwara and Dungarpur in the state of Rajasthan, and in Madhya Pradesh, the districts used in the field study are Neemuch, Mandsaur and Ujjain. Further, both large and small villages are included in the field level observations in the study, as well as single-caste-dominant and mixed-caste villages. The central enquiry of this study is "whether a person's social and economic attributes determined their participation in Gram Panchayat activities" (Ruth J. Alsop et al. 1999).

The study focuses initially on the relationship between people's interest in the Panchayat and voting. According to the field data analysis, the high turnout of villagers in Panchayat elections is not indicative of an overwhelming interest of rural people in the democratic processes of local government. In addition, the study states that the reasons for the high level of participation in elections are social solidarity, the avoidance of tensions within the village, bribery and fear of exclusion and falling below the poverty line. The report highlighted some of the issues regarding people's choice in voting, while stating that the issue is complex, and that some personnel attributes like "education, trustworthiness, age, gender (if female) and broader considerations such as the candidate's household's overall economic and social position, the strength of economic relations between the candidate's household and the voter's household, and bribes paid" may be influential factors in ongoing Grama Panchayat election results (Ruth J. Alsop et al. 1999). The study states that there is a disturbing indication of people's attitude towards the democratic process to change inequitable rural societies: rural communities are more concerned with consolidating existing economic and social relations than using the democratic process towards social inequality in rural areas. It also reported, based on the field responses, that "Grama Panchayats are seen as 'political' bodies, i.e., as organizations dealing with power, not with development. Participation in other political activities related to Grama Panchayats is substantially lower than participation in voting" (Ruth J. Alsop et al., 1999).

As well as its extensive research on the Panchayati Raj system and patterns of participation, S.N. Pattnaik's study raises varied issues concerning women's empowerment and pro-women policies along with women in the Panchayat system. His focus is broadly on women and planned development, empowerment, welfare and development programmes, paying specific attention to the Panchayati Raj System. He opined that "the Constitution of India guarantees to all Indian women equality (Article 15 [1]), equality of opportunities (Article 16) and equal pay for equal work (Article 31 [d]). In addition, it allows special provisions to be made by the state in favour of women and children (Article 15 [3]), renounces practices derogatory to the dignity of women (Article 51 [A] [e]), and also allows for provisions to be made by the state to seek just and humane conditions of work and maternity relief (Article 42)" (Pattnaik, S.N. 2010). In this account it is clear that the government of India has modelled and institutionalised appropriate mechanisms and instruments to achieve a gender just society. He opines that such measures have drastically changed the social, economic and political conditions though some of the traditional social orders that are still trying to exclude women from large social and political affairs.

His analysis includes issues such as workforce participation; land and property rights; crimes against women; sexual harassment; dowries; child marriage; female infanticide; sex-selective abortions; domestic violence and trafficking; and nutritional discrimination, to substantiate the focus on the education and economic development of women. Focusing on existing social and political issues, Pattnaik presents elaborate development programmes and policies to empower women, says that the Indian government has paid much attention to bringing women into mainstream development, and that it has introduced various programmes supporting women becoming part of mainstream society. Further, one of the government's major actions was the introduction of the Constitution (Seventy-third Amendment) Act 1992. This has brought women significantly into grassroots politics.

In the study, he specifically focuses on Karnataka's Panchayati Raj system and shows evidence from the field regarding women's issues concerning PRIs. He opines that the system in Karnataka has brought women into the forefront of politics in general and into stream of decision-making specifically. The study also makes some depressing observations, such as the non-cooperation of ward members and village level officials. In this connection, some case studies are also presented to expose the factual of the matter. For example, one woman elected Sarpanch of the village felt that "I could have achieved a lot more if the others had cooperated" (Pattnaik, S.N. 2010:195). Another case study shows that traditional leadership still has strong influence over grassroots governance and politics, with one such leadership throwing a Dalit woman Sarpanch from office via a no-confidence motion, just because she was a woman and belonged to the Dalit community.

Another report based on grassroots reflections, B.S Bhargava's 'Grassroots Leadership' focuses on the Gram Sabha and how it functions. In Bhargava's view, the Grama Sabha has emerged as an open and public forum for the general review and scrutiny of work carried out by the Panchayat. But the question of whether the Panchayat leadership is involved in open forum and in problem solving is not addressed in this report.

S.N. Mishra, in his study on 'The Seventy-third Constitution Amendment and the Local Resource Base: A Critical Appraisal' reports that the government has taken steps to improve the financial position of the PRIs. However, he states that "the question remains unanswered as to whether these enabling provisions will help to accelerate the improving of the financial health of PRIs. Though sufficient financial resources have been allocated to PRIs, the major question is: how many grassroots institutions have efficiently used them? In this situation, the elected leadership of PRIs and local level bureaucracy need to respond proactively. However, such issues need to be investigated thoroughly.

Studies on Andhra Pradesh

In Andhra Pradesh (A.P), much research work has been done in the form of field studies. The state governments of A.P appointed committees to strengthen the Panchayati Raj institutions; these include the Vengala Rao Committee and the Narisimhan committee (Haragopal, G. and Sudarshanam, G 1995). Structural and institutional changes in the Panchayati Raj system in Andhra Pradesh have been subject to much analysis in the form of books, seminar papers and committee reports. However, most of the work has concentrated on periodical elections and popular participation in PRIs. New ideas are emerging in recent PRI literature: on women's participation, on the reservation of places for the weaker sections of the population, and on special provisions for Sarpanch and deputy- Sarpanch positions in Gram Panchayati elections.

Vasudeva Rao's study focuses on the emerging leadership of women in institutions of local governance. His fieldwork was conducted in three districts in Andhra Pradesh (one from each sub region), namely East Godavari, Khammam and Kurnool. Through these studies, he found that women are uniting through the self-help groups to acquire political power in rural areas.

In Andhra Pradesh, with the self-help group movement in the forefront, women are learning self-management. These groups are strengthening women's unity and enhancing their leadership qualities. In the context of Self Help Groups (Development of Women and Children in Rural Areas) in Andhra Pradesh, Rao finds that, through the mobilization of these groups, women are participating in local bodies as Sarpanches and are becoming effective leaders. In the past, seventy percent of women were unaware of happenings in their communities, but now women's participation in local bodies has increased dramatically (Vasudeva, Rao 2003).

The Economic Weekly's special correspondent's article, focused on 'The Panchayati Raj in Andhra Pradesh' illuminates the issues concerning the Panchayati Raj system and the process of democratic decentralisation, particularly the participation of rural folk in a specific programme of benefit to the village concerned. It notes that there was considerable enthusiasm, mostly self-generated among the villagers. In its initial stages, the system was constituted both with the representation of elected Panchayat presidents and that of "a few non-officials nominated to unrepresented sections, like women, the scheduled castes and backward classes or local 'experts', replacing the previously existing block development committees" (The Economic Weekly 1960:1681).

In the old system, the Block Development Officer (BDO) occupied a prominent role along with a few non-officials, whose roles revolved around the BDO. In this situation, the government of Andhra Pradesh brought organisational and institutional changes in the name of 'democratic decentralisation', for the proper formulation and implementation of programmes of development and to extend the benefits of developmental programmes to local people. This move really changed the scene of local government and governance systems all over the country. It must be noted that Andhra to its credit, set the system up as the people needed it. Other observations made in this study were that, in general, economic benefit was favored over social education, and that in particular, psychological changes were produced affecting villagers' views on social and community welfare. Disputes about the importance of the continuation and upkeep of power at that time are noted.

Roy Kaushik and Rajesh Datta's 'Consultative Study on Synergy between Panchayati Raj Institutions and Self Help Groups' focuses on the nature of the Panchayati Raj system after the Seventy-third Amendment, the relationship between the Panchayati Raj system and the Self Help Group movement, how SHGs were involved in poverty alleviation programmes and how the best SHGs brought about social changes in the three states of West Bengal, Kerala and Andhra Pradesh. However, here the review is strictly focused on Andhra Pradesh, since the national picture has been presented in the previous sections.

In Andhra Pradesh, the study carefully presents a comparison with the Indira Kranti Padham model. Indira Kranti Padham is a programme which emerged from the Society for Elimination of Rural Poverty (SERP), which was supported by the World Bank as part of a poverty reduction strategy. The SERP was set up by the government of Andhra Pradesh to eradicate poverty and improve the livelihoods and quality of life of all of the rural poor families with whom the SHGs were closely involved. Since SHGs were brought into the process of mainstream social change, they were aligned with the Panchayati Raj system in the implementation of rural welfare programmes: these included social security pensions and insurance schemes; wages for labour under NREGS; food security credit via the supply of good quality essential commodities at lower price in the lean agricultural season; dairy intervention; and facilitating the poorest of the poor households in rural areas to purchase productive and ready to use land with assured irrigation (Roy Kaushik, Rajesh Datta, NA).

It is noted that "… they are also providing job opportunities for rural youth and managing fair price shops and Community Managed Sustainable Agriculture (CMSA) to support poor farmers to adopt sustainable agriculture practices that will reduce the costs of cultivation and increase net incomes. They are enabling Collective Marketing to minimize the cost of input to rural poor farmers and to offer remunerative prices for their produce" (Roy Kaushik & Rajesh Datta, NA: 11). Thus it is observed, in this synergy between SHGs and PRIs, that SHGs, as collective citizens, are used by local governments to increase their political strength, and in s democratic system they have emerged as prominent factors in the acquisition of elected power. In addition, each SHG also has its own capability to influence the electoral winning position. It is very important to state that members of SHGs have also emerged as ward members, and that Sarpanches (elected presidents of the Grama Panchayat). Most members also have political affiliations, and it may be understood that SGH members have developed political relationships after the emergence of SHGs.

Bala Vikasa performed an in-depth study on 'Women Elected to the Panchayati Raj in Andhra Pradesh' to examine the factors contributing to women's empowerment and the impact of 'reservation' on the political empowerment of women. The study analyses issues like awareness, roles and responsibilities, responsiveness and reservations. Since empowerment is directly related to awareness, it is observed that some women have knowledge of various developmental programmes of government: issues on women's representation and the roles and responsibilities listed in the Seventy-third Amendment of Panchayat Raj Act. Regarding cooperation, the majority of women have succeeded in fostering the cooperation of political parties for the development of village people. Most of the women and women's representatives failed to attend the meetings at the Gram Panchayat Office due to the influence of their husbands and close relatives. It is observed in the report that "there is more caste discrimination in the case of women, and Panchayat representatives belonging to the scheduled castes and tribes are victims of discrimination and exclusion, irrespective of gender"(Bala Vikasa 2006:30).

Another important issue discussed in the report is that of the factors contributing to women's empowerment. It identifies election contests;

experience as SHG leaders and village committee leaders; and the political reputation of the family, as factors in helping women to emerge as leaders of PRIs. The empirical investigation found problems in the implementation of programmes by women leaders: lack of resources from the government; gender discrimination; lack of cooperation among villagers in the implementation of programmes; caste conflicts and discrimination; and lack of resources. These are some issues that hinder the process of women's empowerment.

E.A. Narayana and S.R. Subhani's research sought to understand the functional aspects. 'Panchayati Raj in Andhra Pradesh: An Appraisal of Some Functional Aspects' specifically focuses on the Gram Panchayat of the Returu of Guntur district. The study highlights efficiency with relation to the educational levels of the elected leadership. It points out that "the poor educational level of leadership is one of the important factors that hinder the success of PRIs". Training and educational standards are said to be essential for the proper and effective functioning of the PRI system. In addition, it is suggested that the state government should make the necessary arrangements for the training of Panchayati Raj non-officials and members belonging to the weaker sections, i.e. SCs, STs, BCs and women who they have entered into PRIs through the reservation system. Narayana and Subhani state the objective of the Panchayati Raj as the development of the concept of participatory democracy at local level. Much success seems to have been achieved, and it is observed that PRI meetings are held regularly, and, in fact, more frequently than required by the statute bodies, and that they are well attended. Based on the findings of the study, it is clear that very few of the intended functions are performed: this is considered to be due to the ignorance of the state government. The research once again emphasizes the need to resolve the problem of devolution of powers and functions, and to allocate sufficient finances (E.A. Narayana & S.R. Subhani 2012).

Studies on Women's Participation and Leadership

Women's leadership in the Panchayati Raj and their empowerment in grassroots politics are emphasized by various scholars, such as P. Manikyamba, Devaki Jain, Thomas W. Hachoegang and others. Manikyamba analyzes the achievements and the shortcomings in the workings of the Panchayati Raj since 1959. She claims that Panchayat Raj institutions have brought about some degree of social change, and that PRIs have increased awareness of the rural people about their rights. Compared to the pre-1959 era, leadership patterns have somewhat favoured new and young people, and the introduction of PRIs has encouraged the emergence of a young, literate leadership. She observes that the economically and socially privileged classes continue to dominate rural politics. It has often been mentioned that these privileged classes hinder the realization of the goals of the Panchayati Raj. She also discusses women's representation in the Panchayati Raj, their awareness and the nature of their participation (Manikyamba, P. 1989).

Dayanidhi Parida's recent research on 'Women and the Panchayat Raj – A Study' is focused on gender equality and the empowerment of women. He explains that women at both socio-economic and political levels have been considered inferior to men in the context of Indian society. While substantiating that, he adds, "family status in the Indian context is judged in terms of male seniority and not of that of the female". Although PRIs have been in operation for decades, women are yet to be accorded equal status by society through Grama Panchayats. Thus, in his opinion, there is a need to strengthen the structural and functional systems of PRIs in order to realize the needs of women's empowerment. Despite the special emphasis placed on women's participation in Gram Panchayats, the study observes that the functions and duties of Grama Sabha are not known to a large majority of respondents. About eighty percent of women are not aware of rural development schemes like NREGS or JRY, or the funds received under these schemes. The reasons for the low level of awareness are identified as dependence on their husbands, low level sof education, lack of interest, inadequacy of training etc.

The study also makes some findings on institutional constraints. In addition, "… reservations for women have led merely to formal, and not to real, empowerment of women in the Panchayats. It is seen that the participation of women shall require the co-operation of their family members. Women do not participate in preparing budgets and plans to the desired extent, and this is unsatisfactory. This is due to less weight being given to women in the patriarchal and male-dominated social system, with its age-old social taboos against women in rural areas". Thus the study clearly shows the challenges to women in the context of the Panchayati Raj (Dayanidhi Parida 2010).

Devaki Jain studies the changing patterns of rural women's participation in decision-making. She finds that women's participation in formal political organizations has been increasing in rural areas since 1995. The study focuses on the state of Karnataka, which passed a law in 1953 providing twenty-five percent of reserved seats for women in local councils. The elections to these councils were held in 1987. She describes the wonderful sight of 14,000 women in the audience, shining brightly, eighty percent of whom were participating in politics for the first time, thrilled with their victory at hosting. Even those who had passed the law and advocated positive discrimination in the interests of gender equality were stunned. Jain observes that women have gained a sense of empowerment by asserting control over resources, officials and, most of all, by changing the views of men. It seems that women have gained self-confidence through local organizations. She further observes that political parties are also encouraging women into formal politics because of their leadership qualities (Devaki Jain 2002).

Virendra Kaur and Sukhdev Singh's field study gives a detailed analysis on the place and role of women in the Panchayati Raj system in the Punjab. They observe that women are increasingly becoming Sarpanches and village presidents. These changes have come through the constitutional provision of reservations for women. The objective of this study is to identify the socio-economic characteristics of women in villages, and their capabilities in decision-making. The study was conducted in the three regions of the Punjab: Majha, Malwa and Doaab. They identify low participation of women in Gram Panchayats despite the special provisions; this is because of male dominance. They suggest that there is a need for attitudinal changes among the males. They also recommend enhancing educational opportunities for women to build their confidence and improve their performance. Some studies evaluate women's empowerment through the recent reforms (Virendra Kaur & Sukhdev Singh 2002).

Snehalata Panda's empirical study based on women in village Panchayats finds that rural women have found space in grassroots institutions, especially in Gram Panchayats in Orissa. Interestingly, the study finds that the women who have entered into grassroots politics are from non-political backgrounds. Further, the reasons for women entering politics are identified as persuasion from family members and, to some extent, requests from neighbours and village communities. An important aspect of this study is that the women who entered into politics with reluctance show great maturity in outlook and enthusiasm, increasing political awareness and perception of their role and responsibility over time.

For example, Santosh Kumar and Arun Deshpande observe that "... the Panchayati Raj system at last made it possible for these historically marginalized people to actively participate in governance." They argue that the bureaucracy, the urban and rural elite, political parties and their leaders view the Panchayati

Raj system with fear as they tend to lose power with emerging new leadership at the village level. Even though the gradual changes in rural leadership and the system encourages all sections of society, especially marginal communities, to participate in village politics, the dominant castes still dominate decision-making at grassroots level (Santhosh Kumar & Arun Deshpande 2002).

Swetha Mishra, in her study on women and the Seventy-third Constitutional Amendment Act, examines the participation of women in the political process and the institutional structure of democracy. In her opinion, the political participation of women is severely limited due to various traditional factors such as caste, religion, feudal attitudes and family status. In her observation, Panchayati Raj institutions have brought rural women into the forefront of village politics. This research study was conducted in the states of Karnataka, Maharashtra, Orissa, West Bengal, Haryana, the Punjab and Madhya Pradesh. In Mishra's findings, women have more opportunities to play a vital role at all levels, including village-level politics, and they need to utilize these opportunities to change the decision-making process (Swetha Mishra 1997).

Roopashri Sinha, Asha Singh and Piyush Bajpai's study of 2002 focuses on women's participation in the improvement of health through the Panchayati Raj. The paper focuses on two villages in Grama Panchayat: Madaripur and Majhauriya in the Lucknow district of the state of Uttar Pradesh. The study attempts a situation analysis to document the status of PRIs, with specific focus on health-providing agencies, women's experiences of participation and the needs they express. The methodology of the study includes secondary data, field observation and focus group discussions. It observes that the president of the village (the Pradhan) has a limited understanding of the PRI system, and that he is dependent on the Grama Panchayat village officer to complete all of the procedures and workings of the Grama Panchayat.

With regard to women in public spheres, especially in Grama Panchayats, active participation is not observed in the locations studied. The women vice-presidents (Upa-Pradhans) of the villages are not active. The study quotes one woman as saying that she could not say anything in the Grama Sabha because her views are also not taken seriously, that women are largely neglected and that their needs for widows' pensions and maternity benefit programmes are not taken into consideration. In one of the study locations, the GP village of Majhauriya, a woman Pradhan was found to be completely dependent on her husband for the regular functions of the Grama Panchayat. It is observed that she herself never attended the meetings of the Grama Sabha, and that her husband always chaired the meetings. Grama Sabha meetings are held and decisions are made, even when the quorum is not complete. The study made some important findings at ground level, such as the insignificance of women's participation in Gram Panchayat meetings, traditional dominance of men over women leaders, and issues relating to their roles in Grama Panchayats and to their social circumstances.

In the context of the Seventy-third Constitutional Amendment, Shashi Kaul and Shradha Sahni examine the extent of participation of women elected representatives in Panchayats and the problems they face. Their study focuses on two districts, namely Jammu and Kathua in the Jammu province. The study explains in detail the political profile: the reason for contesting elections; whether women representatives attend Panchayat meetings; whether they express their views freely in those meetings; whether they face any discrimination in terms of cooperation of male Panchayat members; and their representative capabilities in terms of overcoming constraints, decisions making, functioning in Panchayat administrations, and of their ability to lead.

The study observes significant women's participation in Panchayat meetings, with some members expressing their views very openly and freely, also raising their voices and speaking out on local issues. It is also observed that some of the women's voices were not given adequate attention. The study suggests reasons why women's voices are not heard. The "… main reason is the patriarchal set-up of society, therefore non co-operation" Some existing practical reasons are highlighted in the study: women members feel that there should be no family or community interference in the independent functioning of the Panchayat. Further, "… members complained that they get no assistance or help from family members in the discharge of their domestic work. A majority of the respondents revealed that financial assistance is a necessary ingredient for their self esteem, their independent functioning and their committed concern and approach to the needs and urges of the people of the area." It is observed that family support of women representatives, non-cooperation of other members, community attitudes towards women in leadership, and especially the traditional social system, are dominant in women's political participation in general and in PRIs specifically (Shashi Kaul & Shradha Sahni 2009).

In the context of the Seventy-third Amendment Act, Surat Singh's study on 'Women in Panchayati Raj Institutions: A Study of Participation in the Decision-Making Process' gives a detailed analysis of the position of women in the PRIs of Panchayat Samithis and the Gram Panchayats of Haryana in the decision-making process. The study highlights some important empirical issues. It deals with the interference of husbands in decision making: women are seen to be able to solve problems only in the Panchayat meetings and Grama Sabhas but it is not reported whether they are able to make decisions; very few women leaders enjoy the support of staff in day-to-day functions; their ability to conduct regular meetings is also minimal; they rarely make crucial decisions; the mobilizing of funds is to some extent viable; and information and literacy play prominent roles in decision-making (Surat Singh, 2005).

Women's empowerment has gained momentum in Indian academic circles since the Seventy-third Amendment Act came into force. In fact, the move was initially motivated by a state policy directive which led the government to create a model of decentralized governance (Malik S.S. 2005:181). In line with state policy, various instruments were espoused, such as a community development programme (in 1952); democratic decentralization through the three-tier system of the Panchayati Raj based on the Balwantarai Mehta committee (in 1956); and the constitution of other committees to bring about reform and to encourage women to participate in grassroots politics towards major social change and empowerment. In this context, and on theme of 'Women's Empowerment and the Panchayati Raj', Malik uses the existing literature to seek a concrete understanding of women and their part in politics, of their participation levels, and of government measures.

Malik details how women's empowerment as a major social reform has come into the limelight, and discusses the viability of the concept. His study begins with a viewing of the Indian constitution, with specific focus on the directives of state policy. The philosophical views of M.K. Gandhi and his imagining of India's future are also discussed. For example, Gandhi's commitment to popular governance through decentralization is highlighted. Malik discusses the initial process of women's political empowerment through government initiatives such as the community development programme of 1952 and through various committees: the Balwantrai Mehta Committee (1956); the Ashok Mehta Committee (1978); the C.H. Hanumantha Rao working group on District Planning (1983); the G.V.K. Rao Committee (1985); the L.M. Singvi Committee (1986); the Thungan Committee (1988); and the Panchayati Raj Sammelans (1988-89). He then discusses amendments such as the Sixty-Fourth Constitutional Amendment Bill (1989) and the Seventy-Third Amendment Act (1992), which were subsequently made towards women's empowerment.

In his analysis substantiating his field-based studies, the issues of women's participation in grassroots political activities are discussed: the prevailing male domination, traditional power structures, traditional psychological barriers, caste suppression and hesitation to participate in meetings. He argues that the Seventy-Third Amendment Act has facilitated the reservation system perfectly, bringing women of SCs and STs into public life. But the prevalence of representation by proxy of women's male family members is, in fact a reality, and consequently still women's status of political decision making.

Since women constitute one-third of Panchayat representatives, and since at least one-third of Gram Sabha members at meetings are to be women, it is important that they emerge as new leaders to take up the challenges of their role in tribal politics. Reservation of seats for women, especially for tribal women, will be essential for some years to come, but effort is required to take women's political participation go beyond this level and help to foster a new image of women who can come into politics by themselves and perform independently.

In the final analysis of the review, women leaders have exhibited their determination to occupy the public space, though there are challenges to the process of empowering women. In order to overcome these challenges, it is necessary to sustain the election of women representatives.

It is necessary for women to escape this domination and subordination, and they need to be educated and trained to achieve this. Though these are not in themselves sufficient conditions, if they are not in place women are unable to make important decisions. As well as lack of awareness, education and training, respondents also express opinions on other problems, the most important of which is lack of economic resources. Others include interference by government officials and their non-cooperative attitude, groupism, family problems and traditional values.

To summarize, many scholars agree that the Seventy-third Amendment and the women's movement have motivated a large number of women candidates to stand in local elections. This can be considered an encouraging trend towards women's empowerment. But statutory representation is only the first step in promoting political participation. Studies also show that large numbers of women are yet to be mobilized and that they face many socio-economic and psychological challenges.

Chapter Three

Policy Issues on Panchayat System

The system of self government in Indian villages was widely recognized and deeply characterized by agrarian economies. As George Mathew points out, there is historical evidence of village government systems as far back as 600 B.C. He points out that social connections within villages took the form of Panchayats (assemblies of five persons), which worked to look after the affairs of the village. They had both police and judicial powers, and customs and religion elevated them to a sacred position of authority. As well as the village Panchayats, there were caste-based associations which were prominent at grassroots level. Caste-based associations further ensured that village Panchayats belonging to a particular caste adhered to that caste's code of social conduct and ethics (Mathew, G. 2000). Such historical evidence of significantly socially evolved governing characteristics of village Panchayats were greatly attracted subsequent undemocratic, democratic rulers and governments.

The Panchayat system of the pre-British period was not statutory but voluntary. In that system, the village was the basic unit, and every village had a council consisting of its elders. They dealt with issues and problems that arose locally. This system greatly inspired many rulers and architects of modern governance in India. The British also had interaction with village Panchayats. Sir Charles Metcalfe, a British governor in India in the nineteenth century, even referred to them as 'the little republics'. In fact, local self-government in India, in the sense of being a representative institution accountable to the electorate, was the creation of Lord Ripon in 1882. By 1925, British India had passed acts for the establishment of village Panchayats (Tomar B.S. 1991).

There were the ideological influences of M.K. Gandhi, Dr. B. R. Ambedkar and other philosophers, who partly inspired and influenced government and public leaders with regard to the development of local self-government over the years. As well as these ideological and philosophical influences, the establishment of the Panchayati Raj in all Indian villages was an integral part of the philosophy of the Directive Principles (part IV) of the Indian Constitution (Mathur, P.C. 1995). The introduction of the Panchayati Raj in Indian polity was an attempt at the holistic development and democratization of the villages. However, India's development in the early 1950s was planned without much attention to the Gandhian vision of village republics. The Constitution of India, placing importance on the establishment of a democratic and semi-federal political system, includes Article 40, which relates to the Panchayats. In his chapter on the Directive Principles of State Policy, R.K. Sapru quotes Article 40: "… the state should take steps to organize village Panchayats and to endow them with such powers and authority as may be necessary to enable them to function as units of self-government" (Sapru, R.K. 2010). The following interpretation focuses on the evolution of policies on the Panchayati Raj system.

Policy Measurements of the Panchayati Raj

Since the beginning of the Community Development Programme, policies to strengthen the system of local governance have been given priority, and consequently laws, committees and Acts have been initiated. More recently, the constitutional directives have been interpreted as empowering the government to provide constitutional sanctions for important features, not only of village Panchayats but also of local self-governing bodies, especially of Grama Sabhas.

The Community Development Programme (CDP)

Inspired by constitutional provisions, the government launched the Community Development programme (CDP) in October 1952. Initially, he programme selected fifty-five blocks. The blocks were constituted under the CDP as the primary units in the implementation of development programmes. According to the then Ministry of Community Development of the Indian government, "The initiative for the Community Development Programme comes from the people themselves. Village Communities not only choose the priorities according to which the problems are to be tackled, but they also undertake the major responsibility for implementing them. The role of the government is to assist all of these activities at every stage. Officials guide and help the villagers, provide technical advice and organize supplies, services and finance" (Prabhat K. Mohapatra 2003).

Under this strategy, the Village Level Workers (VLW), as agents of change, were put in place to be involved in all aspects of rural development

(Government of India 1959). Bearing in mind the limitations of the CDP, a further mechanism for its implementation, known as the National Extension Service (NES), was introduced in 1953. Thus the CDP was implemented through the National Extension Service. The difference between the CDP and the NES was that the CDP was an approach, while NES was a method of rural development. In fact, it adopted a 'top-down' method, in which all direction came from the centre, rather than a 'bottom-up' one in which all of the issues would have come from the grassroots. But 'top-down' directions neither reflected local needs nor came with the necessary financial and technical resources. As a result, the programme did not encourage the participation of the local community as expected (Prabhat K. Mohapatra 2003).

The main objective was the development of rural areas. It was observed that there was lack of popular participation in the developmental programmes of rural areas, and the Balwantrai Mehta Committee, which was appointed in 1957 to examine the workings of the Community Development Programme, felt that the reason for its failure was lack of popular interest in the developmental programmes.

The Balwanta Rai Mehata Committee

After the Community Development Project was introduced in 1952, it was realized that without grassroots agency at village level which could represent the entire community and provide the necessary leadership to implement development programmes, real progress in rural areas could not take place. In 1957, the Balwanta Rai Mehata committee's report recommended the establishment of statutory elective bodies. On the basis of this recommendation, a three-tier system of the Panchayati Raj was established in 1959, and almost every state passed legislation to establish Panchayats in the period between 1959 and 1964 (Government of India [Ministry of Agriculture and Irrigation] 1978). The PRIs were conceived as local bodies aiming to ensure the people's participation in development (Government of India, 1959). The committee felt that there was a strong need to create representative institutions to enhance local initiatives, leadership and motivation.

The Balwant Rai Mehta committee report strongly recommended the inclusion of women in the process of local self governance, based on the interest shown by women in the past in the area of women and child welfare (Manikyamba, P. 1989). The real impetus in the evolution of the Panchayat

Raj came in 1957, through the recommendations of the committee headed by Balwantrai Mehta as stated. It was left to states to accept and act upon the recommendations of the committee according to the demands of the situation. Consequently, only a few states established PRIs (Government of India [Ministry of Agriculture and Irrigation] 1978). No uniform structure could be established throughout India on the basis of these recommendations. Even these Panchayats played only a marginal role in the implementation of development schemes, mainly due to the resistance of the bureaucrats. In addition, many factors, such as lack of resources, lack of political support, bureaucratic apathy and the domination of the rural elites, led to the degeneration of Panchayati Raj institutions (Cooperation and Rural Development Department of the Government of Maharashtra 1961:26).

The major recommendation of the committee was the establishment of a three-tier Panchayati Raj system: Grama Panchayat at village level, Panchayat Samiti at block (mandal/taluq) level and Zilla Parishad at district level, with the Panchayat Samiti as the executive body and the Zilla Parishad in an advisory, coordinating and supervisory role. All planning and developmental activities were to be entrusted to these bodies, and genuine transfer of power and responsibility was to be made to these institutions. Adequate resources were to be allocated to all bodies to enable them to discharge their responsibilities properly. All social and economic development programmes were to be channeled through these agencies, and a system was to be developed to effect further dissolution and dispersal of power. The National Development Council accepted these recommendations in January 1958 (Cooperation and Rural Development Department of the Government of Maharashtra 1961).

The Santhanam Committee

The K. Santhanam Committee was appointed in 1963 to look at the financial issues of Panchayati Raj institutions. It recommended that Panchayats should have powers to levy special taxes on land revenues and home taxes, etc.; that people should not be burdened with too many tax demands; that all grants and subventions at state level should be mobilized and sent in a consolidated form to various PRIs; that a Panchayat Raj Finance Corporation should be set up to look into the financial resources of PRIs at all levels; that loans and financial assistance should be provided to these grassroots-level bodies; and also that the non-financial requirements of villages were met. It is significant to note that these recommendations are still in debated in some circles. The committee found that the fiscal capacity of PRIs tends to be limited since rich resources of revenue were claimed by higher levels of government. The Committee was seriously concerned with resolving issues such as the sanctioning of grants to PRIs by the state government, the evolving mutual financial relationships among the three tiers of PRIs, gifts and donations, and with handing over revenue in full or part to PRIs.

The Ashok Mehta Committee

In December 1977, the Janata Government appointed a committee on Panchayati Raj institutions under the chairmanship of Ashok Mehta. The committee submitted its report in August 1978, making 132 recommendations. The main recommendations are as follows: The three-tier system of the Panchayati Raj should be replaced with a two-tier system, with the Zilla Parishad at district level, and below it the Mandal Panchayat, consisting of a group of villages covering a population of 15000 to 20000. A district should be the first point of decentralization under popular supervision below state level. The Zilla Parishad should be the executive body and should be responsible for planning at the district level. There should be official participation of political parties at all levels of Panchayat elections. The Panchayat Raj institutions should have compulsory powers of taxation to mobilize their own financial resources. There should be a regular social audit by a district level agency and by a committee of legislators, to check whether the funds allotted to vulnerable social and economic groups are actually spent on them (Ministry of Agriculture and Irrigation [Department of Rural Development] 1978).

It is strongly recommended that the state governments should not supersede the Panchayat Raj institutions. In case of an imperative supersession, an election should be held within six months of the date of supersession. The Nyaya Panchayats should be kept as separate bodies from the development of Panchayats. They should be presided over by a qualified judge. The Chief Electoral Officer of the state, in consultation with the Chief Election Commissioner, should organize and conduct the Panchayati Raj elections. Developmental functions should be transferred to the Zila Parishad and all development staff should work under its control and supervision. An important role should be given to non-governmental organizations in mobilizing the people's support of the Panchayati Raj. A separate ministry for the Panchayati

Raj should be appointed in the state council of ministers to look after the affairs of Panchayati Raj institutions. Social justice was also given due importance, while reservations were given for SCs and STs on the basis of their population (Ministry of Agriculture and Irrigation [Department of Rural Development] 1978).

Though appropriate actions were taken by the government at that time, it was observed there was slow progress of Panchayati institutions during the 1960s, and they were in decline in the early 1970s for various reasons. Scholars point out that by the 1960s, the strategy for the administration of rural development had itself undergone a change, with greater emphasis now being placed on intensive area development, a 'target group' approach and the 'line' administration of the departmental handling of development. Consequently, another committee was appointed, under the chairmanship of Ashok Mehta, to suggest measures to revitalize the Panchayati Raj institutions. It recommended the removal of the middle level (block) as an administrative unit. However, the idea of a two-tier system was not attractive to state governments: it was rejected by the Chief Ministers' Conference in 1979 and the three-tier system continued (Ministry of Agriculture and Irrigation [Department of Rural Development] 1978).

Further, the process of institutionalization of PRIs gained momentum in the late 1980s. Factors such as the failure of the 'top down' approach to solve the problems of the rural poor had been increasingly recognized by many state governments, development agencies and NGOs since the 1970s. This forced policy-makers and development practitioners to seek alternative strategies based on the principles of social justice, equity, participation and a bottom-up approach. It was also a period during which Centre-State relations was an important issue, with rising regional aspirations and a demand for greater federal polity. Equally, there was an attempt on the part of the Centre to bypass the states and route funds directly to the Panchayats. It was also observed that few resources were reaching the people through bureaucratic filters, and the Panchayati Raj was seen as a mechanism to solve this problem and to extend power and resources to the bottom. The top–down model of development was losing its appeal, and the adoption of the grassroots, bottom-up approach in planning and development became necessary. The government of India was also making the Panchayat Raj the main item on its agenda. All of these issues strongly supported the emergence of the Panchayat Raj (Ministry of Agriculture and Irrigation [Department of Rural Development] 1978).

The G.V.K. Rao Committee

In 1985, the Planning Commission appointed a committee under the chairmanship of G.V.K. Rao to review the existing administrative arrangements for rural development and to suggest an appropriate structural mechanism to activate PRIs. This committee recommended making districts the basic unit of policy planning and programme implementation. The committee decided that rural development must take place and that PRIs must play a central role in handling people's problems. More importantly, it emphasized the necessity of holding regular elections to the Panchayats. The committee recommended that the district should be the basic unit for policy planning and programme implementation, and that regular elections to the Panchayati Raj Institutions must be held. A further suggestion was to establish the block development office to administer the rural development process. Functions such as the planning, implementation and monitoring of rural development programmes were to be assigned to each level of PRI (to district level and below) (Suryanarayana Reddy, R 2012). A Committee for a Concept Paper on Panchayati Raj Institutions (CCPPRI) was constituted under the chairmanship of L M Singhvi to review the functioning of Panchayati Raj institutions in 1987. Importantly, the committee recommended the reorganization of villages, more viable financial resources and the setting up of judicial tribunals in each state to adjudicate in disagreements about relation the functioning of PRIs.

The Constitution (Sixty-fourth Amendment) Bill

Based on previous experience of PRIs and their functioning, a sub-committee of the Ministry of Rural Development was constituted under the chairmanship of P K Thungon in 1988. The sub-committee suggested taking necessary actions through constitutional amendment and as a result, a Constitution (Sixty-fourth Amendment) Bill was modeled in 1989. The Bill was dismissed in the Rajya Sabha as unconvincing (Mohanlal, G.M. 1994: 60). Even so, policy debate about PRIs and their necessity was given importance. The bill also looked at the issues of reservations for women in Panchayats and other local bodies (Sinha, B.K. & Gopal Iyer, K [eds.] 2009: 371).

The Constitution (Seventy-third Amendment) Act 1993

A revolutionary change in the role of the PRIs was brought about by this constitutional act. It established a fully-fledged Panchayati Raj system. The significance of this amendment rests in the fact that it accorded legal status to the Panchayat as a third tier of government, the other two being central and state governments. The seventy-third Amendment recognized village, block and district level bodies and gave them constitutional status under Indian law. At the village level, the most important provisions relating to participation and accountability are those governing reservations and the Gram Sabha. Thus the Act has brought significant changes to the grassroots democratic system (Department of Rural Development of the Government of India 1978: 43).

This change in the Indian political system is the result of a growing conviction that centralized government cannot achieve growth and development in a society marked by an absence of space for the expression of people's initiatives. The significance of the study lies also in the fact that the Seventy-third Constitutional Amendment Act has made it obligatory to hold regular meetings of Gram Sabha, the frequency of which is determined by each state. Another important factor was the boost to the number of women being elected to the three-tier system, an indication of their political empowerment. The Seventy-third Constitutional Amendment created space for women in political participation and decision making at grassroots level by ensuring that one third of the seats are reserved all over the country. The Seventy-third Constitutional Amendment Act 1992 says that it "… provides reservations for women in PRIs set up in two ways: for the office of member, and for that of the chairperson. As per clauses 2 and 3 of Article 243(d), not fewer than one third of the seats for the direct election of members at each tier of the Panchayats are to be reserved for women. Although the percentages of women in various levels of political activity have risen considerably, women are still under-represented in governance and decision-making positions." (Department of Rural Development of the Government of India 1978).

Some major outcomes of the Seventy-third Amendment are as follows: "One-third of all seats must be reserved for women. Likewise, reservations for Scheduled Castes (SCs) and Scheduled Tribes (STs) are made in proportion to their population. The establishment of a three-tier PRI structure, with elected bodies at village, block and district levels, are proposed. (States with populations less than two million are not required to introduce block-level Panchayats.) The recognition is given to the Gram Sabha, which constitutes a deliberative body at the village level. Direct elections to five year terms for all members at all levels will take place. One-third of all seats are reserved for women who are properly initiated. Reservations for SCs and STs proportional to their populations will be streamlined. Similar guidelines are attached to reservations for chairpersons of the Panchayats – Sarpanches. It is optional for state legislatures to provide reservations for other backward groups. A State Election Commission (SEC) will be created to supervise, organize and oversee Panchayat elections at all levels. A State Finance Commission (SFC) will be established to review and revise the financial position of the Panchayats at five year intervals, and to make recommendations to the state government about the distribution of Panchayat funds" (Department of Rural Development of the Government of India 1978).

However, some of the studies note that though the political reservations for women made by Indian parliament, real social issues were neglected by the Bill, because concern was not shown for the women of SC, ST and BC communities. Caste-wise, women's representation was not registered in PRIs. Moreover, upper castes again dominated political space and decision-making bodies. Here I would like to quote from the text of J. Mandal (2003): "It is worth mentioning here the statement of a lady (Chandra Prabha Solanki) at the seminar [on 'Women – Politics and Reservation' at Bombay Bazar] held at Meerut. She said, 'I consider women's demand for reservation a wrong notion, because the reality is that reservations in SCs have not benefited the Dalits, as only the shrewd and affluent Dalits have benefited from it. Similarly, reservation for women will benefit the savarn shrewd and rich ladies. The common women will not benefit. Therefore we should demand all-round facilities for development".

Further, J. Mandal comments that "… the intention behind women's reservations is to capture parliament by installing upper caste women by reducing the reserved seats for SC/ST" and stated that "… reservations for women without allocation of quotas to SC/ST/OBC and minority women will certainly defeat the aim to improve common women, and it will make a permanent supremacy of higher caste women over lower castes and minorities". I definitely accept some important points raised by Mandal on the reservation system and its loopholes concerning the neglect of women belonging to SC/ST/ OBC and minority communities. As of now, prestigious governing democratic political institutions — the Indian parliament — has not made concrete resolutions on social stratification, which is highly influential in Indian political domain. The overall judgment on the effectiveness of the leadership of the

Panchayati Raj in the country by the close of the 1970s was expressed in the report of the Ashok Mehta Committee. It attributed the disappointing impact of the Panchayati Raj to the domination of economically and socially privileged sections of society, political factionalism, corruption and external political interference. After the release of the Ashok Mehta Committee's report during the 1980s, three crucial areas were identified: (a) a focus on anti poverty programme; (b) provision for SCs and STs; and (c) women's participation in grassroots politics (Mandal, J. 2003).

Democratic politics in India encourages only elites to participate in elections, as only they possess the required organizational and material wealth. These are essential for political participation. Unless poor people and women participate in political processes, it is impossible for them to have control over decisions which affect them. To encourage their participation, it is necessary to bring the political system closer to them, which demands democratic decentralization.

At grassroots level, PRIs are supposed to play an important role in the welfare of women. So far, special representation has been given to women in Panchayati Raj institutions through the system of direct elections and nomination to local councils. Recently, provisions have been incorporated to reserve certain elective posts: those of village Sarpanches, Mandal presidents and Zilla Parishads. In this regard, several steps have been taken by the central and state governments. The Seventy-third Amendment Act 1992 is one of the most important steps initiated by central government to give constitutional status to PRIs and to make special provision for deprived classes and for women (Manikyamba, P. 1989).

Provisions of the Panchayats (Extension Scheduled Areas) Bill 1996

Another important Bill was the Provisions of the Panchayats (Extension Scheduled Areas) Bill in 1996. Some important features of this bill are that "State legislations that may be made shall be in consonance with the customary law, social and religious practices and traditional management practices of community resources. Every village shall have a Gram Sabha, which shall be vested with the powers to approve the programmes and projects for social and economic development and also to identify beneficiaries under such programmes. Another important thing is that Panchayats at the appropriate levels shall be endowed with ownership of minor forest produce" (Sinha, B.K. & Gopal Iyer, K. (eds.),2009: 371; http://hppanchayat.nic.in 2012).

Further, keeping the view of traditional management practices, it was given that "… the Gram Sabha or the Panchayat at the appropriate level shall be consulted in the granting of prospecting licenses and leases for the mining of minor minerals, and their prior recommendation will be obtained for the acquisition of land in the Scheduled Areas for development projects or for the resettlement of project affecting members of the Scheduled Tribes. Panchayats at the appropriate level and the Gram Sabha shall have the power to prevent alienation of tribal lands and to take appropriate action to restore any unlawfully alienated land of a Scheduled Tribe; they will have powers to regulate moneylending to members of the Scheduled Tribes, to manage village markets and to enforce prohibition or to regulate or restrict sale and consumption of any intoxicant. State Legislations shall endow Panchayats at the appropriate levels with specific powers and will provide safeguards to prevent Panchayats at the higher level from assuming the powers and authority of Panchayats at the lower level or of the Gram Sabha. The offices of the Chairpersons of the Panchayats at all levels shall be reserved for Scheduled Tribes. The reservation of seats at every Panchayat for Scheduled Tribes shall not be less than one-half of the total number of seats" (Sinha, B.K. & Gopal Iyer, K. (eds.) 2009: 371; http://hppanchayat.nic.in 2012.

PRIs and Five Year Plan Documents

In addition, the Planning Commission was also given due importance to strengthen PRIs through successive five year plans. Since the present study is confined to the study of women in leadership, much of their focus is not emphasized; some of the Five Plan initiatives are presented here. The first and second Five Year Plans focused on CDP, and specifically, the "First Five-Year Plan talked about breaking the National and State plans into local units based on districts, towns and villages. It did not, however, elaborate on how decentralization would be put into operation" (Suryanarayana Reddy, R. 2012). The third Plan attempted to ensure the growth and working of PRIs to enable each area to realize its maximum development potential on the basis of local manpower and other resources, cooperation, self-help, community effort and the effective use of the available resources and personnel (Jathar, R.V. 1964: 571). Consequent Plans also focused on the distribution of financial resources, but the Seventh Plan document (1985-90) re-affirmed faith in the process of decentralization and resolved to proceed on the lines suggested by the Rao Committee.

The Eighth Five-Year Plan (1992-97) was launched on 1 April 1992. It provided a package of structural adjustments in the form of economic liberalization, privatization and fiscal disciplinary reforms. The government recognized that under the evolved system, people had become mere passive observers and receivers of doles. Hence the emphasis was placed on PRI's as the focal point for organizing and implementing rural development programmes. Socio-economic activities like education and literacy, health and family planning, land improvement, minor irrigation, recovery and development of waste-land and aforestation were treated as 'core activities', in which people's participation could be maximized and made more fruitful. The Ninth Plan (1997-2002) required that the PRIs should prepare plans for economic development and social justice toward the integrated development of the district. The Ninth Plan laid emphasis on a comprehensive, time-bound training policy for functionaries in order to equip them with updated information and modern technologies, which in turn were to be disseminated amongst the rural people (Suryanarayana Reddy. R. 2012).

Policy Issues on Reservations for Women in Panchayats

The principle of gender equality is enshrined in the Indian Constitution in its Preamble, Fundamental Rights, Fundamental Duties and Directive Principles of State Policy. The Constitution not only guarantees equality to women, but also empowers the State to adopt measures of positive discrimination in their favour. Since the Fifth Five Year Plan (1974-78), India has made a marked shift in its approach to women's issues, from welfare to development, while keeping the empowerment of women as the central issue in determining their status in society. The National Commission for Women was set up by an Act of Parliament in 1990 to safeguard women's rights and legal entitlements.

Policies for women's political reservations have been the subject of academic debate since the Panchayati Raj Institutions were enforced in the early 1990s. In the 1980s, a number of political developments, particularly the movements and struggles of the emergency and post-emergency periods, led to further debates on women's issues and renewed activity in favour of women. These included an increased focus on women in development in the Sixth and Seventh Five

41

Year Plans, the National Perspective Plan (NPP) for women and the alternative perspective plan offered by the women's movement. In this process of women's empowerment, the Indian government's important constitutional amendment, popularly known as the Seventy-second Amendment Bill of 1990, reserved not fewer than one-third of places for women in membership at all levels, through the legitimized entry of women into PRIs. This was hailed as a major step for inclusive politics, and addressing as it does women's continued political marginality, it has the potential to change existing gender relations.

The Seventy-fourth Amendment of the Constitution in 1993 provided for the reservation of seats for women in the Local Bodies of Panchayats and Municipalities, laying a firm foundation for their participation in decision-making at local levels. Further, India has ratified various international conventions and human rights instruments committing to secure equal rights for women. Significant among them is the ratification of the Convention on the Elimination of All Forms of Discrimination Against Women (CEDAW) in 1993, which also contributed to women entering boldly into political and social spheres; and the Indian government has also made decisions to facilitate this. Recently, at the Third Round Table of Ministers In Charge of the Panchayati Raj, held at Raipur in 2004, some important plans were drawn for the empowerment of women through reservations in Panchayats. Measures included the provision of women's component plans in the budget of the PRIs; links to SHGs; adequate training and capacity-building; encouraging political parties to put up women candidates; the opportunity for women to serve a full term when elected to posts in the Panchayati Raj system; Mahila Sabhas (or their equivalent) to facilitate the raising of women's concerns and issues in Grama Sabha and Ward Sabha meetings (or in the equivalent sub-Grama Sabha); and a separate quorum for women's participation in Grama Sabha and sub-Grama Sabha forums (Sinha, B.K. & Gopal Iyer, K. (eds.) 2009: 493).

Panchayati Raj System in Andhra Pradesh

Initially, the state of Andhra Pradesh's Panchayat Raj structure had its origin in the state of Madras, as it was in Madras at that time. The development of the Panchayat Raj in the state is not an isolated event: it was part of a wider movement to create institutions of local self government that affected the whole country. In 1959, the legislation on the Panchayat Raj was enacted and brought into effect in Andhra Pradesh. As well as central government initiatives such as the Community Development and National Extension services, the state also originated its own village Panchayat system.

The Firka Development Scheme was launched by Tanguturi Prakasam Panthulu, who became Chief Minister of the Madras province when constitutional government was restored in 1946. The Firka Development Scheme was a comprehensive one. Under the scheme, a revenue administrative unit of about thirty villages was set up for the intensive development of rural areas (Government of Madras 1948). The scheme was in operation for period of six years. Then it was replaced in the state by the national initiative popularly known as CDP. Although the scheme did not yield any of the expected outcomes, it brought consensus on development and social change in rural areas (Venkatarangaiah, M. and Ram Reddy, G. 1967).

The Village Panchayat Act of 1950, another important act, came into effect in April 1951. Panchayats now acquired a more democratic character in terms of their functions and powers. However, the Act determined that Panchayats could not function as units of self-government (Madras Rural Development Department 1950). The Panchayats in Andhra continued to function according to this Act even after the formation of Andhra Pradesh in 1956, by integrating the Andhra region with the Telangana region. The Acts of 1950 and 1956 were similar in their functions: there were no differences between them (Panchayati Raj Department of Andhra Pradesh 1959).

In addition to these acts, the remarkable development initiation popularly known as the Community Development Programme (1952) was in operation, and the National Extension Service was added in 1953. These gave an added advantage in bringing more focus onto the creation of local governments. With these programmes in operation, the government of the state of Andhra Pradesh issued a white paper on rural local development, and meanwhile accepted the recommendations of the Balwantarai Mehta Committee in their entirety. However, before legislation was undertaken to implement these recommendations, the scheme was trialed in twenty blocks with the setting up of Panchayat Samithis. Experience of these ad hoc Panchayats was positive, and based on this the government introduced the Andhra Pradesh Panchayat Samithis and Zilla Parishads Act, which came into force with effect from 1 November 1959 (Panchayati Raj Department of Andhra Pradesh 1959).

This Act underwent several amendments over time, and some important legislations were enacted to bring about the effective functioning of the PRIs. In 1961, an amendment was made to the Panchayat Act, enhancing land access and increasing the number of standing committees from five to seven.

Another important act was the Andhra Pradesh Gram Panchayat Act of 1964. This act allowed the reservation in the first instance of two seats for women if the total membership of the Gram Panchayati was nine or fewer, three if it was between ten and fifteen and four if it was more than fifteen (Mishra & Singh 1993). Thus the Act ensured that women were represented at between twenty-two and twenty-five percent in grassroots politics through the Grama Panchayat elections.

Further to this, the state government appointed committees such as the Vengal Rao Committee (1968) and the Narasihman Committee (1971) to look into the existing system of PRIs. Though these committees made some recommendations, the state government accepted only two of them, amending both the Panchayat Raj Acts in 1978. These recommendations were to directly elect presidents of Panchayati Samithis and Gram Panchayat Samithis on the basis of universal adult franchise, and to continue the three-tier system of PRIs. Thus the three-tier system of the Panchayati Raj came into being, and this continued until 1986. Then, a new act brought in major structural changes. The acts prior to 1986 had recognised that there was no provision for women's reservations.

The Act of the Seventy-third Amendment made structural changes and created a new type of mechanism known as the Mandal Praja Parishad. Since the Gram Panchayat was confined to a village, the Sarpanches (presidents), Upa-sarpanches (vice-presidents), MLAs and MPs were made ex-officio members of the Mandal Praja Parishads. Subsequently, the structure of the Panchayati Raj system was further deepened by the Andhra Pradesh Panchayati Raj Act (Act No. 13 of 1994) based on the Constitutional Seventy-third Amendment Act of 1993. According to this Act, a Gram Sabha should conduct meetings twice a year. It envisages the Gram Sabha as the centre of all activity at grassroots level. The Sarpanches (chairpersons) are directly elected by the people at village level. The village Panchayat is divided into different wards; from each ward, one member is to be elected directly to the Gram Panchayat by the voters of that ward. Then the Upa-sarpanch (vice chairperson) is elected by the elected ward members.

The Act of 1993 brought more representation in PRIs for women. The proportion of women at Grama Panchayat level was 33.84 percent, at the Panchayat Samithi (SP) level, it was 37.01 percent, and at the Zilla Parishad (ZP) level, it was 33.38 percent increased (Smitha, K.C. 2007). Thus the act has to some extent demonstrated changes in women's participation in the decision-making process in grassroots governance. According to the Government of

Andhra Pradesh Panchayati Raj Act 1994, the three-tier structure of PRIs includes the Gram Panchayat at the village level, the Mandal Parishad at the middle level and the Zilla Parishad as the highest institution at district level. A Grama Panchayat consists of between five and twenty-one ward members depending upon its population and on the Sarpanch. The ward members and Sarpanch are directly elected by the voters of the village. Members of the Grama Panchayat are elected for a term of five years, and the elections are conducted by the Andhra Pradesh State Election Commission. Elections to Grama Panchayats are not conducted on a political party basis, but candidates are generally associated with and supported by political parties. As the act recommends, there are reservations by rotation for Scheduled Tribes, Scheduled Castes, the Backward Classes and women. The reservations for the Scheduled Castes and Scheduled Tribes are based on their proportions in the population, whereas reservations for the Backward Classes are given at thirty-four percent, and one-third of the total seats are given to women in all categories including the open category.

The Grama Panchayats are divided into two types based on the income of the village, namely Notified Grama Panchayat (Major Grama Panchayats) and Non-Notified Grama Panchayats (Minor Grama Panchayats). Of a total of 21,943 Grama Panchayats in the state of Andhra Pradesh, 1,472 are recognized as notified and the remaining 20,471 as non-notified.

As a middle level Panchayati institution in the three-tier system, a Mandal Parishad is constituted for a revenue Mandal. A Mandal Parishad is comprised of members of the Mandal Parishad Territorial Constituency (MPTCs); the Legislative Assembly (MLAs); those with jurisdiction over the Mandal; the councils of states who voter in the Mandal; and one co-opted member from a minority group. Members of the MPTC are directly elected by territorial constituency voters, and the president of the Mandal is elected in turn by MPTC members. Members are elected for a term of five years, with elections conducted on a political party basis by the State Election Commission. The Sarpanches of the villages in the Mandal are permanent invitees to the meetings of Mandal Parishad. Rules of reservation are applied as in the Grama Panchayats and Mandal Parishads.

At the top level of the system of PRI are Zilla Parishads (ZPs). These consist of members of the Zilla Parishad Territorial Constituency (ZPTC), MLAs and those with jurisdiction in the District. They also include members of the Council of States who are registered voters in the District, and two co-opted persons belonging to minorities. As with Ward Members at the

Grama Panchayat level and MPTCs at middle level, elections to the ZPTC are conducted directly, with the chairperson elected in turn by members of the ZPTC. Members are elected for a term of five years on a political party basis. Presidents of Mandal Parishads are permanent invitees to Zilla Parishad meetings. A similar reservation system is in place for Scheduled Castes, Scheduled Tribes, the Backward Classes and women.

The Act has transferred diversified powers to these various-level institutions, such as the planning and execution of programmes for rural development. These include communications, provision of drinking water, minor irrigation and poverty alleviation programmes. Prominent activities of PRIs, including Grama Panchayats, are the maintenance of secondary, upper primary and primary schools in rural areas; the maintenance of minor irrigation tanks with ayacuts of up to 40 hectares; the construction of school buildings; the provision of basic civic amenities to people living in their respective villages; and maintaining the Panchayat's roads and other assets. The main financial sources for developmental activities are Grants-in-aid and Finance Commission Grants, and there are other local sources of revenue for PRIs, such as House Tax, license fees levied by Grama Panchayats etc.

Women in Grassroots Level Organizations

In addition to PRIs, women have other opportunities to enter into public life. The scope to do so is provided through grassroots-level committees which were formed to streamline people's participation in developmental activities and programmes. There are various committees, such as the Joint Forest Management (JFMs) Committees; the Village Education Committees (VECs); the Water Users' Groups; the Village Organization of Self Help Groups (SHGs); SHGs themselves; Mandal Samakhyas; and Mothers' Committees. Though male dominance is visible in JFMs, VECs and the Water Users' Groups, committees exclusively for women have been formed and found to function well; these include the Village Organization of Self Help Groups, SHGs, Mandal Samakhyas and Mothers' Committees. These multiple committees are expected to encourage more involvement of the people and more benefits from the government. Women see them as opportunities to ensure their participation in the development of their villages through their involvement in a large number of government programmes. Scholars have said that the bureaucracy, too, favours these committees since it is able to have a greater say in the implementation of programmes through these committees. Committees focusing on specific issues, be it education, health or forest management, can take note of the specific objectives of the programme and deliver better results. It is expected that in the long term, members of these committees will also be elected as members of the Panchayats.

However, leadership of women in Grama Panchayats is not yet a visible reality. But it is now widely recognized that effective leadership by women is both desirable and possible. Until the Panchayati Raj came into villages, there were no opportunities for women to become leaders, but some recent trends in states like Andhra Pradesh and Karnataka reveal the emergence of new young women's leadership. Recently, some field studies of women's leadership within the Panchayati Raj system has suggested that the women's participation in Panchayati politics has been increasing since the 1970s. Some academics and activists, like Misra, Kaur and Singh and Manikyamba, have noted that some women leaders were very active and committed. This situation is definitely an encouraging one, but despite the introduction of institutional mechanisms for the political empowerment of rural women, caste issues and traditional male dominancy still impact negatively on the decision-making power of women leaders.

Chapter Four

Socio-Politics and Area of the Study

The present chapter presents a profile of the study area, starting with the Nizamabad district in which the villages of Srirampur and Chittapoor are located. It is useful to know about the environmental factors of the study area, such as place, climatic conditions, population, socio-economic conditions, political processes etc. Knowledge of the socio-economic conditions of the district will facilitate an understanding the leadership capabilities of the respective villages.

I. Profile of the Nizamabad District

The Nizamabad district is situated in the northern part of the state, and is one of the ten districts of the Telangana region in the state of Andhra Pradesh. It is bound on the north by the Adilabad district, on the east by Karimnagar, on the south by the Medak district and on the west by the Bidar district of Karnataka and the Nanded district of Maharashtra. It lies between 18-5 and 19 degrees of northern latitude and between 77-40 and 78-37 degrees of eastern longitude. The geographical area covers 7,956 square kilometers i.e. 1,980,586 acres, spread over 923 villages in thirty-six mandals, of which 866 are inhabited villages, with fifty villages that are either uninhabited or submerged under irrigation projects (http:// nizamabad.nic.in/code/profile. accessed on 02/08/2003).

The Rivers Godavari and Manjeera are the predominant rivers of the district. These provide water for nearly sixty percent of the district's agricultural land. The district's main river is the Godavari, which flows for around 113 kilometers on the northern boundary and serves Karimnagar's agricultural land. The river Manjeera rises in Patoda Taluqa in the Bidar district of Karnataka, crosses the Nizamabad district from south to west and joins the Godavari near the village of Kandakurthi in the Renjal mandal of the Nizamabad district (The Government of Andhra Pradesh 1995).

48

This district's multi-purpose dam is the Sriram Sagar project, constructed on the river Godavari at the village of Pochampad in the Nizamabad district. It flows down to the Karimnagar and Adilabad districts and to some parts of the Warangal district. Only twenty-three villages in the Nizamabad district, covering 1,394 hectares, benefit from this project. There has been reduction in its storage capacity resulting from silt formulations, and repairs have had to be made to the canal system of these twenty-three villages. The project also has a hydroelectric power station with an installed capacity of 3x9 M.V.A (The Government of Andhra Pradesh 1995).

The district's second major irrigation project is the Nizamsagar project; this is on the River Manjeera near the village of Achampet in the erstwhile Banswada Block. This project also has a hydro-electric power station with an installed capacity of 3x5 M.V.A. There are other, smaller irrigation projects in districts such as Pocharam, Ramadugu and Nallavagu. Agriculture is the backbone of the district's economy, with about eighty-one percent of the workforce dependent on it. The main crops grown are rice, sugar cane, maize, turmeric, cotton, groundnuts, sunflowers and pulses.

Patterns of Land Use

The district is not rich in minerals. Its few economic minerals are building stones, clay ore, manganese ore, mica, semi precious stones, talc and soap stones, with iron ore of poor quality occurring in a few places as lateritic capping and ferruginous quartzites. The district's hills are situated in the table land of Deccan; hills of considerable range are quite rare. The forest covers an area of 1.69 lakh hectares, covering twenty-two percent of the total geographical area of the district (The Government of Andhra Pradesh 1995).

Social Composition of the District

At the 2001 census, the total population of the district was 23.42 lakh. The population of rural areas accounts for 19.20 lakh, and the urban population thus accounting for 4.22 lakh. Of the total population, 11.62 lakh are male and 11.8 lakh are female. The district occupies an area of 7956 square kilometers with a density of 257 people per square kilometer. Its literate population is

5.96 lakh. The total S.C. population of the district is 3.08 lakh, while S.T. population accounts for 1.21 lakh.

The working population of the district is about 10.14 lakh. Participation in work in the agricultural sector is higher for women than for men. The female work participation rate in the agriculture sector in the district has significantly increased, from 67.69 percent at the 1991 census, to 89.1 percent by 2001(http://nizamabad.nic.in/code/profile, accessed 02/08/2003).

The people of the district belong to different castes and religions, including Scheduled Castes and Tribes, Backward Castes, Hinduism, Islam and Christianity. Generally, economic potential is considered a major factor in the dominance of some sectors over others. Caste and class also play a dominant role in social relations in the region. Dominant caste groups include Kamma, Kapu and Reddies. These castes play an active role in the district's social, economical and political life and they also predominantly control the district's land and business.

Political Profile of the District

Since independence, the Congress Party had a strong hold over the district's political activity up until 1980-81. In 1982, when the Telugu Desam was established, political allegiance shifted towards this newly formed regional party. Telugu Desam secured an overwhelming majority in the Panchayat, Assembly and Parliamentary elections. As well as these political parties, there are trade unions and Communist and Marxist groups, which also effectively work as pressure groups.

Very recently, the Telangana Rashtra Samiti (TRS) emerged with the concept of separate Telangana statehood. This party is backed by the Velama community. Other parties such as Bharathiya Janatha, the Communist Party of India, CPM, and CPM (ML) also have influence in the region. Various Naxalite groups' activities have been spreading rapidly in the district over the past fifteen years. There are also several student and youth organisations working actively in district politics. The Congress Party is mainly backed by the majority of the Reddy community. The Kapu and Kamma groups support the Telugu Desam Party; and many of the backward caste and SCs STs are supporters of the political parties and groups on the left.

Functioning of the PRIs

The Panchayati Raj system in the Nizamabad district is three-tier, as it is all over the state of Andhra Pradesh. There is one municipal corporation (Nizamabad), two municipalities (Kamareddy and Bodhan), thirty-six mandals and 719 Grama Panchayats. The leading elected representatives are known as Sarpanch at village level, President of Mandal Praja Parishad at mandal level and Zilla Parishad (ZP) Chairman at district level. Sarpanches are elected by the people directly, Mandal Parishad Presidents (MPPs) are elected by Mandal Parishad Territorial Constituencies (MPTCs), and ZP Chairmen are elected by Zilla Parishad Territorial Constituencies (ZPTCs). There are 922 general villages and sixty-one uninhabited villages as well as Grama Panchayats.

II. Profile of the Study Villages

From the selected district, the villages of Srirampur and Chittapoor were selected as samples for in-depth study. A brief profile of these villages is presented here.

Srirampur

Srirampur is a small Grama Panchayat village in the Balkonda Mandal in the district of Nizamabad. It is situated on National Highway No. 7, 32km from Nizamabad and 182km from the state capital, Hyderabad. The village was relocated due to its being submerged in the Sriram Sagar irrigation project (popularly known as the Pochampad project) in 1975. Prior to that project, it was, in fact, a major village. It had extensive irrigational facilities including tanks, canals, river flow (from the Godavari) and ground water with fertile agricultural land. There were, at that time, agro-based rural industries including rice mills and other small-scale artisan businesses. When it came to relocation, plots for houses and agricultural land in the Karimnagar district were initially allotted to this village, but the people did not agree to this, and they themselves found the present location and bought their own plots and land. However, most of the economically forward classes and some of the backward classes did not settle in the present village, but went to other large villages, and others settled in the towns and cities as their economic capabilities allowed. Those who were economically and socially weak settled in the present village, a small hamlet of the major Grama Panchayat of Chittapur. This continued until a separate minor Gram Panchayat was formed in 1994. Even the village became a separate Gram Panchayat; however some government records, especially land records, are retained by the Grama Panchayat of Chittapur.

Area and population

The total geographical area of the village is around 225 acres, of which only 43.14 are used for the village settlement; of the settled area, 178 acres are used for agricultural purposes. The main sources of irrigation are submersible pump sets. About sixty acres of land is not cultivatable because of lack of irrigation facilities. The population of the village (according to the population's own account book, dated 25/06/2001) is 589, comprising 257 males and 332 females. In terms of social hierarchy, the Scheduled Caste population is 256, with 165 males and 191 females. The total Backward Caste population is 195, with ninety-two males and 103 females. The number of other caste members is thirty-eight, with eighteen males and twenty females (Janabha Record of Grama Panchayat Office, Srirampur 25/06/2003).

Social Composition of the Village

In this village SCs are divided into the two sub-castes of Mala and Madiga Backward Castes groups are also divided into sub castes such as Tenugu (fruit sellers), Kammari (goldsmiths), Shaala (tailors), Chaakali (washer men), Gouds (toddy tappers), Gundla (fishermen), Komati (traders), Mangali (barbers) and Chindula (street dancers). There is no higher caste population in this village; there are no Reddy, Kapu or other Forward Classes. The village leaders support the two major political parties i.e. the Congress and Telugu Desam Parties. There are other caste organizations for young people, namely Ambedkar Yuvajana Sangham and Shivaji Yuvajana Sangham. In addition, there are seven women's self-help groups of the DWCRA, and men are organised into Rythu Mithra Sangams, groups working for the social and economical development of the village.

DWCRA women in the village play an active and assertive role. They participate effectively in the political affairs of the village during the Grama

Panchayat elections. In addition, these groups support women who stand in Grama Panchayat elections. In the 1994 Grama Panchayat elections, they supported a woman for the Sarpanch seat, and thus returned a woman leader. Thus, male control of Grama Panchayat politics is being challenged by women's groups. The Srirampur Grama Panchayati consists of ten ward members, of which four elected members are women.

Cropping pattern

Rice, maize and turmeric are the major crops in the village. Details of areas under these major crops and the yield per acre are given below.

Infrastructural facilities

The village has a primary school, an Anganwadi centre, a Grama Panchayat building, a library, a branch post office, four hand-operated bore wells and now changed them into submersible pump sets by attaching single phase motors, three submersible pump sets, one major drinking water tank (capacity 75,000 litres) and three minor water tanks for drinking water. The village acquired an electricity supply as late as 1981. It has a total road length of 6km, of which 2km road is constructed from cement and concrete.

Chittapoor

Chittapoor is a major revenue Grama Panchayat village in the Nizamabad district. It is also located on National Highway No. 7, thirty-seven kilometres from Nizamabad and five kilometres from Balkonda, Mandal Revenue Office.

Area and population

Chittapoor covers an area of 2,152 acres. Of this area, 750 acres are constituted of village lakes known as Grama Cheruvu, Chintala Kunta and Gupuru Kunta; 500 acres of land is under state government control and 30.3 acres land belongs to ceiling land. The village settlement covers nearly eighty acres and the remaining area is used for agriculture (Land Record Namuna No. 3, Grama Panchayat of Chittapoor, District Nizamabad, A.P. 2000).

There are 550 households in the village, with a population of 2,579 persons (1,249 males and 1,330 females). The most numerically dominant group is the Backward Caste, numbering around 1,820 (881 males and 939 females); the politically and economically dominant caste group is Munnuru Kapu, which together with other Forward Castes, has ninety-one members (forty-eight males and forty-three females); while the Scheduled Castes (Mala and Madiga) consist of around 668, with 336 males and 332 females. The remaining population belongs to other groups such as Muslims and Christians (Grama Vikasa Darshini, Gram Panchayat of Chittapoor, District Nizamabad, A.P. 2000).

Social structure

The population of the village is comprised of different caste groups such as Munnuru Kapu, Gundla, Tenugu, Mala, Madiga, Chindula, Mere, Vyshya, Chaakali, Patkari, Aarre, Kammari, Kummari, Ousali (goldsmiths) Mangali, Gouds, Chenchula, Vaddera, Reddies, Brahmanas, Golla and Muslims.

Village organizations

This village consists of caste organisations, women groups, farmers' organizations, youth associations and others, such as the Educational Development Committee, the Mothers' Committee, the Water Users' Committee, the Watershed Committee and the Forest Development Committee. These developmental committees work under the Grama Panchayat office of Chittapoor.

Cropping pattern

The main crops grown in the village are rice, maize, turmeric, vegetables and other oil seeds. The village's irrigation mostly depends upon submersible pump sets: although there are lakes, they are not suitable for agriculture.

Infrastructural facilities

The village has a separate Grama Panchayat building called the Grama Sachivalayam (the village secretariat), a high school, a library, a post office and a sub telephone exchange. The village's drinking water depends upon submersible pump sets and hand bore pump sets. It has a total road length of around 10km, of which 400 metres is constructed with cement and concrete. In this village, eight tractors, owned by upper caste people are used for agricultural works.

Political aspects

In the political scenario of the village, three major political parties, Congress, Telugu Desam and Telangana Rashtriya Samithi, have notable presence. All of these enjoy support from the dominant Munnur Kapu community. There are also party political rivalries among the Backward Caste and Scheduled Caste people, who support the Congress, TDP and TRS parties. The Panchayat of Chittapoor is divided into ten wards, with three women ward members, and the present Sarpanch (in 2004) is from the backward community.

Chapter Five

The Character of Elected Representatives

In this chapter we focus on emerging leadership opportunities and on women's roles in Grama Panchayat politics. Leadership is an important aspect of the Panchayati Raj system. An understanding of the socio-economic and political background of leaders is essential to an assessment of leadership capabilities: the capacity of leaders is considerably influenced by socio-economic and political factors (Madan, N.Z. 1989).

The socio-economic factors that impact on women's political potential include personal factors, familial factors and social status. In addition, organizational affiliations with women's self-help groups, the DWCRA and other labour organizations such as Beedi workers' organizations, also enhance women's confidence.

Personal Factors

Age and gender are identified as the two important personal factors associated with participation in politics (Manikyamba, P. 1989). Personal political experience is very important for candidates to gain access to power structures. Age influences power politics at all levels, including at Panchayat level.

The age distribution of members is shown in Table 5.1. 42.5 percent are between thirty-six and forty-five years old, while thirty-five percent are between twenty-five and thirty-five. Only 22.5 percent of members are over forty-five. Among women members, 45.46 percent are forty-six and above, while 36.36 percent are from middle-aged women (thirty-five to forty-five). The remaining 18.18 percent are young women of twenty-five to thirty-five. It has been observed that there is inadequate representation of younger women members in the Gram Panchayat elections. This is certainly detrimental to women being brought into the decision making process of grassroots politics.

Education

Education is not an important factor in Indian politics; however, sometimes it does influence a person's political participation. Duverger is convinced that education is the most decisive factor in women's political participation. The above study indicates the relevance of education in politics. The level of education of respondents is important in the understanding of the political scenario in their localities in particular and in India in general.

The educational backgrounds of the respondent are shown in Table 5.2. Of the total respondents, fifty percent of respondents have had no formal schooling, and thirty-five percent have attained a high school-level education. Here, a small number (only fifteen percent) of respondents have a college-level education. On the other hand, of the total female members, only 47.3 percent have up to high school education, and the remaining 52.7 percent of women respondents are non-literate.

Another significant factor is that there are no female participants with college-level education. Among male respondents, almost fifty percent have no education background. From this information on the educational status of members, it can be observed that at the Gram Ganchayat level, there are still members who are non-literate, and this non-literacy is most prevalent among women. The educational level of women in rural communities needs to improve, mainly for reasons of rural leadership, because education widens the outlook and enables a person to understand the needs of the people.

Occupations

Political participation in Indian politics is very much influenced by occupation. Particlarly in rural areas, landlords and high-income persons dominate rural politics (Ijlal Anis Zaidi, S.M. 1988). Occupation is an important factor not only in rural politics, but also in state and national politics. In India, the traditional dominance of politics by lawyers is declining, and their place is being taken by farmers and agriculturists. In Andhra Pradesh, whether in Panchayat, Assembly or Loksabha elections, the recent trend is that agriculturists dominate.

Information on the occupational status of respondents is gathered and presented in Table 5.3. Here, 62.5 percent are engaged with agriculture as their main occupation, while only 7.5 percent of respondents are engaged in village-level business as their chief occupation. Thirty percent of members provide other services, including daily wage labouring, driving, toddy tapping, etc. Table 5.3 shows that 61.54 percent of women work in agricultural and allied services as daily wage labourers. Only 38.46 percent of women respondents work in other services such as beedi making and building construction. In these villages, women participate in agricultural work significantly more than men, who work in the fields only during harvest times. This reflects the fact that women work hard at household work, agricultural work and other daily labour sectors.

Land Holding

A democratic political system aims to abolish social divisions and establish equality, which means that no person will be treated better or worse on the basis of their income. In rural areas, the local-level political power structure is characterized by the domination of the landed class and its allies over the class of the landless (Rajendra Singh 1970). Thus, mostof the villagers have traditionally been excluded from power structures in the villages of India. For this reason, it is important to know the respondents' landholding system.

Respondents are categorized on the basis of the size of their families' land in Table 4. It may be seen that of the forty respondents, thirty percent are landless people, while 37.5 percent own land of between one and three acres. In India those with up to three acres of land are categorized as small-scale farmers. Most small farmers belong to the Scheduled Castes and backward classes. Twenty percent of landowning respondents have between three and five acres, while 12.5 percent have more than five acres.

Caste

Caste and religion are dominant factors in Indian public life (Narang, A.S. 1987). The elections for Panchayats, Municipalities, Assemblies and even Parliament show that the caste influence is fairly strong. In fact, the Panchayati Raj system has strengthened the caste system.

The caste distribution of respondents in Table 5.5 shows that 67.5 percent of members belong to backward castes, while thirty percent are from Scheduled Castes and the remaining 2.5 percent of members are from other castes.

According to these data, women from the two villages comprise only 32.5 percent of members, and comparatively speaking, the percentage of female participants is higher in Srirampur than in Chittapoor.

Political Participation

The purpose of this section is to understand the political backgrounds of leaders at grassroots level. Their affiliation with political parties is significant in this context. A Gram Panchayat leader's membership of a political party is an indication of that leader's ideological commitment on the one hand, and the political party's role in the village on the other.

Respondents are classified according to their political party affiliations in Table 5.6. An overwhelming majority of sixty-five percent belong to the Congress party, with twenty percent of respondents supporting the Telugu Desam Party. Very recently, the Telangana Rashtra Samiti (a regional party) has also acquired the support of a few Panchayat leaders (12.5 percent), and the remaining one person (2.5 percent) belongs to the Bharatiya Janata Party. A very high percentage of female Panchayat leaders support the Congress party (84.62 percent), and a very small percentage belong to Telugu Desam Party (TDP) (15.30 percent). There is no participation of women in the Bharatiya Janata Party (BJP) and Telangana Rashtra Samithi (TRS) parties.

It is obvious that all Panchayat leaders support political parties. All of the parties aim to increase the participation of backward classes, Scheduled Castes, tribes and women's communities in Panchayat Raj institutions. It is clear that Panchayats accept the involvement of political parties into their system: political parties provide financial and public support to Panchayat level leaders during elections. This analysis shows that most Panchayat leaders belong to Scheduled Castes or other depressed classes. Also significant is that the Panchayat system encourages young, educated women into the decision-making process.

Chapter Six

Women Leadership: Issues and Challenges

This chapter is devoted to an analysis of the general perceptions and opinions of respondents on women in leadership. It also aims to analyze the functioning of women leaders in their villages, with regard to development programmes taken up by women Sarpanches and ward members. The entire chapter is based on primary data collected by interviewing forty elected Gram Panchayati leaders, of whom thirteen were women. The questionnaire includes both closed and open ended questions.

To find out about respondents' perceptions on the functioning of women leaders, we asked, "Have women leaders brought visible changes in village development?" The opinions expressed fall into three broad responses: (1) Yes, women leaders have brought about visible changes in some areas (including the provision of drinking water, the development of village roads, sanitation, loans, health facilities, educational facilities, libraries, electricity supply, irrigation, agricultural development etc.); (2) No, women leaders cannot bring visible changes in their respective villages; and (3) No response.

According to our data, the majority of the respondents (sixty percent) feel that women leaders have brought visible changes (Table 6.1). According to these respondents, the female Sarpanch has introduced many welfare schemes, such as Deepam, through which almost forty gas cylinders were sanctioned to the Scheduled Castes and Backward Castes by women of the DWCRA. Under the DRDA (District Rural Development Agency), she provided four sewing machines for Backward Caste women and four automobiles for unemployed youth. Moreover, she built a drinking water tank with a capacity of 75,000 litres, and introduced Pucca house loans for poor people under the Ambedkar Awas Yozana scheme. The woman Sarpanch also built a new Gram Panchayat office, a school building and a school compound wall with funds from the Jawahar Rojgar Yozana and the Tenth Finance Commission. Also, she has tried to get medical facilities for her village.

Almost thirty percent of respondents disagree that women's leadership is effective. In their view, female leaders have not brought about any visible changes. They claim that the new developments were only possible because of male effort, and that the female leaders have been dependent on their husbands. Twenty percent of respondents had no opinion on the matter.

A comparative analysis of the two villages regarding women in leadership shows that in Srirampur, an overwhelming majority of seventy percent felt that female leaders are effective and consider them to be capable persons in matters of village development. But in Chittapoor, only 52.17 percent of respondents place importance on female leaders. A general observation can be made that the respondents here consider female leaders to be ineffective in village development as well as in women's welfare.

In answer to the question, "Do you think that the strength of female leaders in the village Panchayats is satisfactory?", as many as 47.5 percent of respondents replied positively (See Table 6.2). Only ten percent of them gave no response. However, some variations are evident in female leaders' responses that there is inadequate representation of women. Women respondents think that state and central governments should accept responsibility for increasing the number of women in power. They also say that the reservation system has not been functioning properly. These perceptions indicate the need for state and central governments to implement effective provisions for women's representation in all Panchayat bodies.

Next we looked at the reasons for the inadequate representation of women in village Panchayats. Only women respondents were asked about this. In their opinion, women's families were not allowing them to enter politics because of their conservative social values. Another reason for inadequate representation involved the traditional headmen. Each caste community is represented by one person, an elder who is economically and socially influential. There are five or six headmen for each village, and these traditional leaders do not accept women in leadership. Therefore, the traditional attitudes of the people regarding women's participation in politics need to change. Women's own indifference needs to be overcome. According to present data, women are educated only to tenth grade standard. Compared to men, their educational status is very poor. However, this can be overcome through effective special provision for women in rural India.

Further social constraints hinder women's empowerment in Gram Panchayats. Village politics in India is dominated by the traditional landed and upper caste people. This leadership has not granted opportunities to any of the marginalized sections, such as Scheduled Castes, Tribes and women. Traditional rural leadership, then, is the main social obstacle to women empowerment in rural politics. This indicates that only people's attitudes and government policies can change women's status in grassroots politics.

We asked the question "In your experience, what are the challenges that women face as Panchayat leaders?" of women only (Table 6.3). Almost sixty percent agreed that traditional headmen and Panchayat officers such as village secretaries and Mandal-level officials neglected women in leadership. These women leaders feel very bad about their responsibilities, but despite the problems they face from village headmen and officials, women still actively participate in grassroots politics.

The response to the question "Do you focus on women's issues such as midwives, family clinics and drinking water in your village?", is positive (Table 6.4). 67.2 percent of respondents are focused on basic needs for women, such as widows' pensions, proper drinking water systems, medical facilities through Mandal health assistants and subsidized loans for families headed by women. Female leaders in Gram Panchayats have raised the issue of wages for agricultural and beedi-making labourers: agricultural labourer's wages have increased from Rs. 25 to Rs. 40 per day, and those of beedi making labourers have risen from Rs. 21 to RS 35 per thousand beedies. It is observed that women leaders have also provided for basic requirements to be met, especially for women. Women have proven themselves to be effective leaders and have disproved the notion that they are silent spectators at Panchayat-level politics.

To find out about women's participation in other associations and developmental groups, such as DWCRA self-help groups, we asked, "Are you associated with any women's groups?"(Table 6.5). One hundred percent of respondents are members of DWCRA groups and political parties. They believe that self-help groups strengthen economical as well as political conditions in the villages. According to these women, political parties support women in Panchayat elections because women outnumber men in the villages. Obviously, a political party wants support from the majority of the population, and political parties are seen to prefer women to participate in village politics.

To find out respondents' opinions on leadership, we asked, "Leadership is important for village development: what kind of leadership do you think is good?" Forty percent of respondents feel that party-based leadership is effective for village development (Table 6.6). They claim that political parties distribute money in elections and encourage public support for participants in village-level politics. Respondents believe that party-based leadership can secure funds for necessary facilities in villages. On the issue of whether female leaders bring visible changes in the respective villages, thirty-seven percent feel that developments like road construction, drinking water and loans to poor people are brought about by women. However, 22.5 percent still prefer male leaders to female ones. It is interesting to note that the Gram Panchayat members accept that party involvement and women leadership are important to village development.

To assess village leaders' efforts to meet basic needs in their Gram Panchayats, we asked, "As a Gram Panchayat leader, do you fulfill the basic needs of villagers?" The answers, presented in Table 6.7, show that an overwhelming majority of ninety percent of women and men responded positively. In Srirampur, most agree that all elected Gram Panchayat members, including women, come together to make decisions regarding village development. On the other hand, Chittapoor respondents report that they make such decisions individually.

To further probe the interests of respondents regarding their involvement in Gram Panchayat politics, we asked "How did you get involved in politics?" Forty percent replied that they made the decision to enter Gram Panchayat-level politics independently, 22.5 percent were persuaded by friends, 17.5 percent were asked by a political party, and twenty percent of respondents became involved on the initiative of the people. (Table 6.8).

Thus, it is evident that most respondents decided to engage in village politics on the initiative of friends and family members. In particular, women ward members and Sarpanches got into politics through their family support only; very few of them came up through the political party initiatives.

To gauge respondents' perceptions of the utility of village Panchayats, we asked, "Do you agree with the view that the Panchayati Raj system has brought about satisfactory improvement in conditions for the villagers (Table 6.9). An overwhelming majority of respondents, both women and men, consider that the Panchayati system has brought visible benefits. An insignificant proportion (ten percent) responded negatively, disagreeing that Panchayats are developing rural areas. The remaining ten percent gave no response.

Though most respondents agree that the Panchayati Raj system works effectively in villages to bring about development, they also raise some issues regarding Gram Panchayat development funds, partial distribution of welfare schemes such as civil supply cards and draught pensions, and other agricultural loans. Despite this negative response, nearly eighty percent of the people agree that the Gram Panchayat facilitates many necessities such as the construction of a Panchayat office and a primary school, a new sanitation system, short-term agricultural loans, the supply of seeds through the Gram Panchayati office, and so on.

To gain insight on the general condition of women in the Panchayati Raj system, we asked: "Do you agree with the view that the establishment of the Panchayati Raj system has brought about satisfactory improvement in conditions for women?" (Table 6.10). As many as fifty percent of respondents believe that the Panchayati system has brought about social, economical and political improvements in conditions for women. A female respondent explained, "We (women) did not enter into Gram Panchayati office until a separate Gram Panchayat was formed, but now not only do we enter the office, we have discussions with Panchayati Raj higher officials. Also, we make decisions regarding village development". In our research, one important finding is that self-help groups are emerging as pressure groups in village politics. Also, Gram Panchayat-level female leaders gain moral support from these groups during and after elections. It seems that women, too, are concerned about political and economical development issues.

Another question we put to the respondents was "How much progress has there been in village development work since the establishment of the Panchayati Raj system?" Table 6.11 shows that about sixty percent of respondents feel that much progress has been made in the village, in the form of the construction of drainage systems, maintenance of proper street lighting, a regular drinking water supply, the construction of Pucca houses for poor people and so on. Twenty percent of the respondents claim that the introduction of the Panchayati Raj system has brought about only small changes in the villages. The remaining twenty percent are skeptical about any progress brought about by Panchayati Raj institutions.

To find out respondents' general perceptions on the distribution of welfare schemes for rural poor people, some specific questions were asked, such as, "Do you agree with the view that the benefits of the Panchayats' development work are felt by poor people?" (Table 6.12). The response was positive: fifty percent agree that the Panchayat system has benefited villagers living below the poverty line, with 37.5 percent disagreeing. There appear to be wide differences of opinion about whether most of the benefits, other than public utilities, go to those few who can establish political power in the villages. 12.5 percent gave no response to the question.

The Gram Panchayat members in the sample were elected to their positions in 1994 and 2001. It is, therefore, necessary to know their opinions regarding political parties and their participation in Panchayat elections. The following question was asked of Panchayat members to assess their participation in political parties: "Were you a member of any political party at the time of the election?" (Table 6.13) About ten percent of respondents were found to belong to political parties. Of these, as many as sixty-five percent belong to the Congress party, twenty percent to Telugu Desam and 7.5 percent to Telangana Rashtra Samithi (TRS). Of the total female respondents, 76.82 percent belong to the Congress party and 23.18 percent to Telugu Desam. There are no women candidates from TRS. It is a widely held opinion that political parties play an active role in Gram Panchayat elections, even though they are not officially recognized, and no party symbols are allotted to candidates.

In response to the question "Do you realize that the Panchayat is divided into groups?" (Table 6.14), the majority of respondents (92.5 percent) admit that their Panchayats are divided into factions. 7.5 percent did not answer this question. Table 6.14(a) shows that quite a substantial majority of respondents feel that, since the Panchayati Raj system has come into existence, each village has been divided into rival groups.

According to Table 14(a), as many as fifty percent of respondents feel that Gram Panchayat leaders create division in villages in order to win Sarpanch and Presidential elections. Others (almost thirty-five percent) feel that political party loyalties and traditional rivalries have a divisive impact. Some respondents also state that elected Panchayat members work for their own interests, while those who could not get elected form opposition groups. Individual, family and caste differences are prominent in elections.

Summary

This analysis shows that the majority of respondents appear satisfied with women's leadership within their villages. The Panchayati Raj system in rural areas has brought about qualitative changes in the form of political, economical and social improvements. Many respondents feel that there are enough women in Gram Panchayat elections, though special provisions are still necessary to empower them. The general feeling of women respondents seems to be that women leaders continue to face challenges from traditional leaders, who have do not consider them to be legitimate leaders. Sometimes government officials also neglect women leaders in Gram Panchayat offices.

However, women leaders, as Sarpanches and ward members, fulfill villagers' basic needs such as drinking water, road construction and health facilities. Despite male dominance and the dominance of the upper castes, a positive climate has been created for women in leadership by the Seventy-third Amendment Act and by the self-help groups. Most respondents also agree that the establishment of the Panchayat system has brought about satisfactory improvements in conditions for villagers in general and women in particular. However, they also feel that the Panchayati Raj system has failed to make a positive impact in some areas, such as the continuing hold of the traditional leaders, factionalism and excessive party interference in Panchayati elections.

Chapter Seven

Conclusion

After India's Independence, the first and foremost committee, towards equality of women, was constituted in 1975 to review the legal, economic, social and political status of Indian women. The committee reported that women's views were not reflected in any of the Parliament or in Legislative bodies because many women were not elected. Even then, the Committee did not recommend for reservation of seats for women either in the Parliament or in Legislative Assemblies. However, it recommended constituting all-women panchayats to look after the welfare of the women. In 1988 on the other hand, the National Perspective Plan for Women (1988- 2000) recommended for thirty percent seat reservation for women at all levels of panchayats to increase their visibility in public space (Bidyut Mohanty, 2003). The committee has felt that the reservation of seats for women in the grassroots political institutions became necessary because the national thinking to strengthen the panchayats had already started. It was also thought that once the women become successful leaders at the grass roots level, their presence in the Parliament and Assemblies would automatically increase.

Panchayats (traditionally panchayat is an institution in which decisions regarding social issues in the village are taken by five wise men of the village) are not new to India. Some of the studies viewed that the participation of people in the election of panchayats is high but high voter turnout was not indicative of an overwhelming interest in the process of democracy of local government. The influential factors of decision making in the election are social solidarity, avoidance of tension within the village, bribery, fear of exclusion from below poverty line lists and often simply the thrill of participating in the festival of elections.

Though the concept of Panchayat Raj is well known to rural people and active participation of government officials and elected members has enhanced general interest in the gram panchayat politics in recent years, effectiveness and efficiency much to be improved. Functional and institutional issues like financially viable, involvement in micro level planning, functions, powers and resources, regular elections of gram panchayats in regular intervals, allocation of funds and strengthening grama sabhas are yet to be strengthened. Still social inequality was visible in the contexts of periodical village assembles, regular elections and in terms of sufficient representations of weaker sections of society like SC's & ST's and women.

Leadership is a strong and important element in any society which leads society into better and prosperous societal landscapes. Leadership is an essential feature of all government and governance. Leadership secures prosperity in the long run; foolhardy leadership may bring about a catastrophe. Leadership is a crucial element in making people participates in the process of change. The vision and perceptions of leaders play a powerful role in engaging the populace. Leadership is quite indispensable in influencing people to cooperate towards a common goal and to create situations for collective response.

Formal leadership in a village is enjoyed by those who hold any official position such as membership in the panchayat bodies; but villagers attach greater importance to informal leaders than to formal leaders. A man who is called upon to settle disputes or to discuss village problems is regarded as an informal leader whether or not he enjoys any official position.

Leadership as a concept deals with personnel character and individual ability to make follow his/her supporters as he/she wishes for change. How can we understand leadership in political domain is also noteworthy to discuss here. Leaders in all situations and contexts need to communicate a culturally resonant vision beyond their merely self-interested career goals. Political leadership, the art of initiating collective agency and directing oneself and one's followers, overlaps significantly with the higher levels of military, judicial, organizational, religious and ideological leadership. Political leadership is a part of social leadership in general, but its boundaries are difficult to delimit because of cultural and regime contexts in which it is contextualized.

In a democracy, power is legitimated through popular electoral mandates, and leadership is based on the popular will. In the context of democracy in India, such mandate has been continuously enshrining and new factors like caste and social mobility has emerged as very important factors. In political terms, periodic elections and rule of law are in and of themselves proving much better instruments in changing the reality of the citizens especially with respect to gender inclusivity. In the current system, people serve the political leadership. Based on the existing literature political leadership is connected with ethical and cultural character, the traits and ethical-cultural character of the followers with whom the leader interacts.

Leadership of women in PRIs, some studies brought positive changes. Though, political affairs like factional disputes continuing in dominating village politics were hindering women leadership. In such scenarios, some committees have expressed the need to restrict the hold of political parties in PRIs and on the contrary, the Santhanam committee explicitly recommended that there should be no legal provision prohibiting political parties from influencing panchayati raj elections. These committees suggested that political parties should be inhibited from nominating candidates for panchayats and allotting party symbols for different candidates in the panchayat elections. The Siddiq Ali and Santhanam committees recommended that political parties should not be recognized for the purpose of panchayat elections. Possibilities such as disallowing political parties from participating in elections and in the operation of panchayati raj bodies, applying pressure for unanimous elections, promoting consensus in the working of Panchayati Raj institutions and making panchayats as politics-free zones, have been suggested in various seminars and conferences. In contrast, the study by B.S. Bhargava emphasised that successful functioning of Panchayati Raj system depends to a great extent on the role of political parties and the nature of politics generated in the system.

As regards to Women's Empowerment as a major social change issue, women's entry into the local political bodies at village level panchayats through the 33 percent reservation system which was provided by the Constitutional (73rd Amendment) Act, 1992 was largely discussed and brought grass-root level observations based on the empirical investigations.

The 73rd Constitutional Amendment Act has been hailed as a revolutionary step towards decentralization of power and governance. The amendment provides for the village assembly i.e. the Grama Sabha (GS). It also ensures uniformity in terms of tenure. Administrative units and all states are obliged to conduct periodic elections by an autonomous body. The Amendment gives constitutional status to village, block and district level bodies under the Indian Constitution. Moreover, the Gram Sabha (GS), as a basic democratic unit of India, has given due importance and strengthened its institutional process by providing compulsory and regular direct elections to five year terms for all members at all levels, one-third of all seats are reserved for women, reservations for SCs and STs proportional to their populations and chairpersons (Sarpanches) of the Panchayats are among others.

Further, the Act also constituted institutionally a three tier system of Panchayati Raj for all States having population of over 20 lakh, regular elections (every 5 years), and appointment of State Finance Commission to make recommendations as regards the financial powers of the Panchayats and constitution of District Planning Committees to prepare development plans for the district as whole. As per the Constitution (73rd Amendment) Act, the Panchayati Raj Institutions have been endowed with such powers and authority as may be necessary to function as institutions of self government and contains provisions of devolution of powers and responsibilities upon Panchayats at the appropriate level with reference to the preparation of plans for economic development and social justice; and the implementation of such schemes for economic development and social justice as may be entrusted to them.

The significance of the amendment is that it provided reservation of seats for women, SCs and STs at all levels including the village, intermediate (Mandal, taluka/Block) and district panchayats (Manikyamba, P. 1989). As a result, a common system of governance that aims for actual people's participation has been introduced in all the states of the country. In short, an attempt has been made to realize Mahatma Gandhi's concept of gram Swaraj through the Panchayati Raj act. Consequent upon the enactment of the Act, almost all the States/UTs, except Jammu & Kashmir, National Capital Territory of Delhi and Uttaranchal have enacted their legislation. As a result, According to the Report of the Ministry of Rural Development (2002), 2,32,278 Panchayats at village level; 6,022 Panchayats at intermediate level and 535 Panchayats at district level have been constituted in the country. The report has also argued that these panchayats are being manned by about 29.2 lakh elected representatives of Panchayats at all levels.

But, recent literature (e.g. Crook and Manor, 1998; Jha, 1999; 2000; Mathew, 2001a; Mukarji, 1999; Oommen, 1999; Vyasulu, 2000; World Bank, 2000a and Smitha, 2007) on these institutions have argued, the ambiguity surrounding the concept of 'self-government' and power to local people, especially in decision making power that still rests with the State governments have prevented most States from devolving any substantive power to the Panchayats. Such findings are consistent with a wider literature on the problems most commonly associated with decentralization in India.

Review of literature has concluded that women's political career especially at grass-root politics, depends upon cooperation and support of family members and collaboration between husband and wife. It is clear that without support of husband, women cannot enter into politics and it is essential for women. Further, women mostly depends husband's good rapport with the people and his association with political party at the time of elections.

In Andhra Pradesh SHGs were involved rigorously in grama panchjayat politics and SHGs supporting women brought into mainstream political process. In addition there is strong synergy between SHGs and PRIs, SHGs as collective citizens are used by local government for implementation of politically strong and in democratic system they have emerged as prominent factors in acquiring elected power. Some studies highlighted the state responsibilities in strengthening of function of panchayati raj through trainings, power and financial allocation and devolutions.

The Seventy-third Constitutional Amendment Act 1993 has given priority for the reservation of seats for members of Scheduled Caste, Scheduled Tribes and women both at the membership and functionary level. This effort was meant to create conditions favourable to democratic decentralization through wider participation (Ibid). In general the emergence of Panchayati Raj has brought visible changes in Srirampur and Chittapoor villages in the form of roads, health facilities, drinking water etc., but there are several problems still continuing at grassroots politics in India in general and in the study villages specified in particular. In this research we found out some of the problems faced by gram panchayats. The smooth functioning of the panchayats is being disturbed by hurdles like inadequate financial resources (to maintain proper facilities of Gram Panchayats), misuse of welfare funds, domination of bureaucracy over elected panchayat leaders as most of the elected members have no literacy.

Regarding women leadership, constitutional provisions, government policies, social action plans and awareness of rural women together have provided women with necessary skills to enjoy equal opportunities. The Panchayati Raj has provided a common forum for social, economic, political and legal advancement of rural women. Now women are more than nominal members in the panchayat bodies and this is an epoch-making step in the women's empowerment and political participation.

In our research, we found that women's leadership and their capacity are being praised by the people of the two villages and especially by women. In our observations and conversation with elected members of gram panchayat, women's unity and co-operation together strengthened their confidence in grassroot politics. Chintala Vanaja one of my respondents, said that "I got immense support from my DWCRA members during panchayat elections and won MPTC with their support". We can understand, through this statement, that only with women support she got tremendous majority in elections. There we can say that men and women both equally accepted women leadership for their future development directions.

In our research, it became clear that DWCRA groups are emerging as influential political force in gram panchayat elections. Mr. N. Chandrababu Naidu, Chief Minister of Andhra Pradesh, praised the DWCRA groups in political and economical terms as "largest force of its kind in the world" (the Hindu, 6 December, 2003). These groups are strengthening women's unity in political, social and economical arena. In these two villages so far, DWCRA groups saved nearly Rs 3 lakhs, including revolving funds. This money capital is earning more money through interests; this money has been given to farmers, village level traders and those who needed loans, thus women are getting opportunity to control politics apart from traditional and land lordship politics.

Even though the Panchayati Raj system brought about visible changes in the condition of villages especially women, still there exist institutional, social and psychological obstacles. Some general orientations and social norms impose restraints on women participation and performance. Consequently, women tend to remain in peripheral roles even when they have special provisions in village politics. Some women are still deteriorating themselves their grade due to lack of education and awareness.

Some women feel that they are only meant for household work. One respondent said, "If we took active participation in politics in Panchayat Raj our family will be broken". Some active members of gram panchayat said that their views were neglected by male members and officials. They were not even allowed to express village problems. Women leaders are still hesitating to attend gram panchayat meetings and sit in front of aged and politically experienced persons.

Economically sound and aged traditional village leaders literally reject the concept of women's entrance into grass root politics. According to their opinion women should not come out from home and women don't know how to handle village problems. Besides, village headman system is dominating over elected panchayat leaders irrespective of gender. According to the headmen of village women should not come to public sphere, they should not hold any office chair. But in recent political scenario in villages the traditional and headmen leadership was neglected by political parties because political parties want their strength in quality and quantity.

Political parties such as Congress, Telugu Desam Party, BJP and other regional political parties were trying to get women and new young people's membership. Especially women and political parties are getting confidence, cooperation and support during elections by working together. One woman respondent said "we have got support from political parties in the form of money and muscle power; otherwise we would have been dominated by other landlords and economically sound people."

However, women leaders desired changes in the form of psychological and institutional transformation in village panchayats. "Vijayalaxmi, who was the first woman sarpanch of Srirampur village, said "While I was working as a sarpanch, I had faced obstacles from panchayat officials, they didn't even consider my applications, which were only for the sake of village people. Often I used to bring my husband to mandal revenue office because without my husband they used to neglect me." This sort of attitude has to be changed. Another institutional change has to be taken for better functioning of gram panchayat that economical independence and more financial assistance has to be provided. Otherwise development of village would be deteriorated. One woman said "Whenever gram panchayat meeting was conducted, we used to have argument with each other for funds distribution for our ward's development". It seems lack of financial resources result to conflicts among panchayat leaders.

Here are some suggestions that need focus for the better involvement of women in Panchayati Raj Institutions such as requirement of attitudinal change in both men and women. There is a feeling that women are meant for household activities and bearing children needs to be replaced by a feeling of equal partnership of women and men. To inculcate this, they should be imparted education for bringing about social and political awareness among both. There should be increased emphasis on ensuring the participation of women in the meetings of Panchayats at all the levels, especially at Grama Sabha level. This is needed to promote and enhance their leadership qualities and self-confidence. It will help them to perform better in the Panchayats and to ensure their participation in the meetings. Attendance of all women must be made compulsory from Gram Panchayat to Zilla Parishad for effective participation and participation in decision-making process. The Grama Sabha is basic unit of effective democratic system which needs to be strengthened through active participation, regular functioning with proper provisions. The proper provisions in conducting Grama Sabha are sensitization, awareness, information and participation. These important issues are lacking, based on the present study, highly missing. Therefore, effective leadership from women community will appear at the grass root, especially Grama Panchayats and in Grama Sabhas soon with proper socio-political and democratic provisions.

Since women constitute one-third of the panchayat representatives and also since, at least one-third of the gram sabha members in the meeting are to be women, it is important that they emerge as new leaders to take up the challenging role in tribal politics. Reservation of seats for women, especially for tribal women is essential for some more years, but efforts are required to ensure that women's political participation go beyond it which will help to foster new image of women who can come into politics themselves and perform independently. In the final analysis of the review women leaders have exhibited their determination to occupy the public space, though there are hurdles in the process of empowering women. In order, to overcome the hurdles need to make the 'empowerment process', and sustainable the elected women representatives.

It is necessary that women come out of this domination and subordination for which they need to be educated and trained. Though these two are not sufficient conditions in themselves, their dearth prevents women from taking important decisions. Besides lack of awareness, education and training, the respondents also expressed their opinions regarding other problems. Lack of financial or economic resources was considered as the most important one. Interference by government officials and their non-cooperative attitude, groupism, besides family problems and traditional values, were other problems.

Tables and Graphs

Chapter-4

Figure 1.

(In lakh ha.)

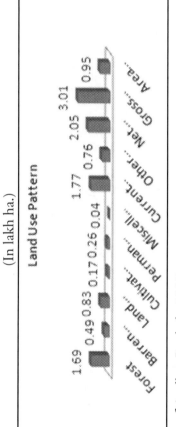

Land Use Pattern

Source: The Government of Andhra Pradesh, 1995

Table 4.1 (In quintals)

S.No.	Crop	Area	Average Yield
1.	Rice	38	53.20
2.	Turmeric	12	52.30
3.	Maize	98	180.00
4.	Vegetables and Oil seeds	30	50.00

(Source: Village level Field Data, 2 March 2003 to 31 May 2003)

Tables of Chapter-5

Table – 5.1: Distribution of members in Grama Panchayats by age

Age	Name of the villages								
	Srirampoor			Chittapoor			Total		
	Women	Men	Total	Women	Men	Total	Women	Men	Total
25-35	2 (28.57%)	5 (50%)	7 (41.18%)	0 (0.00%)	6 (35.29%)	6 (26.07%)	2 (18.18%)	11 (40.74%)	13 (35%)
36-45	4 (57.15%)	2 (20%)	6 (35.29%)	2 (33.34%)	10 (58.82%)	12 (52.16%)	6 (36.36%)	12 (44.44%)	18 (42.5%)
46 and Above	1 (14.28%)	3 (30%)	4 (23.53%)	4 (66.66%)	1 (5.88%)	5 (21.30%)	5 (45.46%)	4 (14.81%)	9 (22.5%)
Total	7 (100%)	10 (100%)	17 (100%)	6 (100%)	17 (100%)	23 (100%)	13 (100%)	27 (100%)	40 (100%)

Table- 5.2: Distribution of Panchayat Members on the basis of educational level

Educational status	Name of the villages								
	Srirampoor			Chittapoor			Total		
	Women	Men	Total	Women	Men	Total	Women	Men	Total
No formal Schooling	4 (57.14%)	4 (40%)	8 (47.05%)	4 (66.66%)	8 (47.05%)	12 (52.17%)	8 (52.70%)	12 (44.44%)	20 (50%)
Up to High Scholl	3 (42.85%)	4 (40%)	7 (41.17%)	2 (33.34%)	5 (29.41%)	7 (30.43%)	5 (47.30%)	9 (33.35%)	14 (35%)
Collage level	0 (0.00%)	2 (20%)	2 (11.76%)	0 (0.00%)	4 (23.52%)	4 (17.39%)	0 (0.00%)	6 (22.23%)	6 (15%)
Total	7 (100%)	10 (100%)	17 (100%)	6 (100%)	17 (100%)	23 (100%)	13 (100%)	27 (100%)	40 (100%)

Table -5.3: Distribution of Gram Panchayat members according to occupation

Occupation	Name of the villages								
	Srirampoor			Chittapoor			Total		
	Women	Men	Total	Women	Men	Total	Women	Men	Total
Agriculture	3 (42.85%)	5 (50%)	8 (47.05%)	2 (33.33%)	8 (47.05%)	10 (43.47%)	5 (38.46%)	13 (48.14%)	18 (45%)
Agri-labour	3 (42.85%)	3 (30%)	6 (35.29%)	2 (33.33%)	3 (17.54%)	5 (21.73%)	5 (38.46%)	6 (22.22%)	11 (27.5%)
Other Business	0 (0.00%)	1 (10%)	1 (5.88%)	0 (0.00%)	4 (23.52%)	4 (17.39%)	0 (0.00%)	5 (18.51%)	5 (12.5%)
Others	1 (14.28%)	1 (10%)	2 (11.76%)	2 (33.34%)	2 (11.76%)	4 (17.39%)	3 (23.07%)	3 (11.11%)	6 (15%)
Total	7 (100%)	10 (100%)	17 (100%)	6 (100%)	17 (100%)	23 (100%)	13 (100%)	27 (100%)	40 (100%)

Table – 5.4: Distribution of Gram Panchayat members in terms of land-holding

Land holding	Name of the villages								
	Srirampoor			Chittapoor			Total		
	Women	Men	Total	Women	Men	Total	Women	Men	Total
Land less	3 (42.85%)	4 (40%)	7 (41.17%)	3 (50%)	2 (11.76%)	5 (21.73%)	6 (46.15%)	6 (22.22%)	12 (30%)
1 – 3 acres	4 (57.14%)	5 (50%)	9 (52.94%)	1 (16.66%)	5 (29.41%)	6 (26.08%)	5 (38.46%)	10 (37.03%)	15 (37.5%)
4 – 5 acres	0 (0.00%)	0 (0.00%)	0 (0.00%)	0 (0.00%)	8 (47.05%)	8 (34.78%)	0 (0.00%)	8 (29.62%)	8 (20%)
6 & more acres	0 (0.00%)	1 (2.5%)	1 (5.88%)	2 (33.34%)	2 (11.76)	4 (17.39%)	2 (14.31%)	3 (11.11%)	5 (12.5%)
Total	7 (100%)	10 (100%)	17 (100%)	6 (100%)	17 (100%)	23 (100%)	13 (100%)	27 (100%)	40 (100%)

Table – 5.5: Distribution of Gram Panchayat according to caste

Caste	Name of the villages								
	Srirampoor			Chittapoor			Total		
	Women	Men	Total	Women	Men	Total	Women	Men	Total
SCs	5 (71.47%)	5 (50%)	10 (58.82%)	0 (0.00%)	2 (11.76%)	2 (8.69%)	5 (38.46%)	7 (25.92%)	12 (30%)
BCs	2 (28.51%)	5 (40%)	6 (35.29%)	6 (100%)	15 (88.23%)	21 (91.30%)	8 (61.53%)	19 (70.37%)	27 (67%)
Others	0 (0.00%)	10 (100%)	1 (5.88%)	0 (0.00%)	0 (0.00%)	0 (0.00%)	0 (0.00%)	1 (3.70%)	1 (2.5%)
Total	7 (100%)	10 (100%)	17 (100%)	6 (100%)	17 (100%)	23 (100%)	13 (100%)	27 (100%)	40 (100%)

Table – 5.6: Political party wise distribution of Gram Panchayat members

Party wise categories	Name of the villages								
	Srirampoor			Chittapoor			Total		
	Women	Men	Total	Women	Men	Total	Women	Men	Total
Congress	5 (71.47%)	7 (70%)	12 (70.58%)	6 (100%)	8 (47.05%)	14 (60.86%)	11 (84.63%)	15 (55.55%)	26 (65%)
T.D.P	2 (28.51%)	3 (30%)	5 (29.41%)	0 (0.00%)	3 (17.05%)	3 (13.04%)	2 (15.38%)	6 (22.22%)	8 (20%)
T.R.S	0 (0.00%)	0 (0.00%)	0 (0.00%)	0 (0.00%)	5 (29.41%)	5 (21.73%)	0 (0.00%)	5 (21.73%)	5 (12.5%)
B.J.P	0 (0.00%)	0 (0.00%)	0 (0.00%)	0 (0.00%)	1 (5.88%)	1 (4.34%)	0 (0.00%)	1 (4.34%)	1 (2.5%)
Total	7 (100%)	10 (100%)	17 (100%)	6 (100%)	17 (100%)	23 (100%)	13 (100%)	27 (100%)	40 (100%)

Tables of Chapter-6

Table 6.1: Have women leaders brought visible changes in village development?

Response	Name of the villages									
	Srirampoor			Chittapoor			Total		
	Women	Men	Total	Women	Men	Total	Women	Men	Total
Yes	7 (100%)	5 (50%)	12 (70.58%)	6 (100%)	6 (35.29%)	12 (52.17%)	13 (100%)	11 (40%)	24 (60%)
No	0 (0.00%)	4 (40%)	4 (23.52%)	0 (0.00%)	8 (47.05%)	8 (34.78%)	0 (0.00%)	12 (45%)	12 (30%)
No Response	0 (0.00%)	1 (10%)	1 (5.88%)	0 (0.00%)	3 (17.64%)	3 (13.04%)	0 (0.00%)	4 (15%)	4 (20%)
Total	7 (100%)	10 (100%)	17 (100%)	6 (100%)	17 (100%)	23 (100%)	13 (100%)	27 (100%)	40 (100%)

Source: Field Study

Table 6.2: Do you think that the strength of women leaders in the village Panchayats is satisfactory?

Respone	Name of the villages								
	Srirampoor			Chittapoor			Total		
	Women	Men	Total	Women	Men	Total	Women	Men	Total
Yes	3 (42.85%)	6 (60%)	9 (52.94%)	2 (33.33%)	8 (47.05%)	10 (43.47%)	5 (38.46%)	14 (51.85%)	19 (47.5%)
No	4 (57.14%)	4 (40%)	8 (47.05%)	4 (46.67%)	5 (29.41%)	9 (39.13%)	8 (61.53%)	9 (33.33%)	17 (42.5%)
No response	0 (0.0%)	0 (0.0%)	0 (0.0%)	0 (0.0%)	4 (23.52%)	4 (17.39%)	0 (0.00%)	4 (14.81%)	4 (10%)
Total	7 (100%)	10 (100%)	17 (100%)	6 (100%)	17 (100%)	23 (100%)	13 (100%)	27 (100%)	40 (100%)

Source: Field Study

Table 6.3: In your experience, what are the challenges that women face as Panchayat leaders? (women leaders only)

Statements	Name of the villages			
	Srirampoor	Chittapoor	Total	
Problems from village people	4 (57.3%)	0 (0.00%)	4 (30.76%)	
Obstacles from officials	2 (28.5%)	0 (0.00%)	2 (15.38%)	
From both sides	1 (14.2%)	6 (100%)	7 (53.84%)	
No response	0 (0.00%)	0 (0.00%)	0 (0.00%)	
Total	7 (100%)	6 (100%)	13 (100%)	

Source: Field Study

Table 6.4: Do you focus on women's issues such as midwives, family clinics and drinking water in your village? (women leaders only)

| Response | Name of the villages | | |
	Srirampoor	Chittapoor	Total
Yes	5 (77.5%)	4 (66.6%)	9 (67.2%)
No	0 (0.00%)	0 (0.00%)	0 (0.00%)
No response	2 (28.5%)	2 (33.4%)	4 (32.8%)
Total	7 (100%)	6 (100%)	13 (100%)

Source: Field Study

Table 6.5: Are you associated with any women's organisations or group (women leaders only)?

Response	Name of the villages		
	Srirampoor	Chittapoor	Total
Yes	7 (100%)	6 (100%)	13 (100%)
No	0 (0.00%)	0 (0.00%)	0 (0.00%)
No response	0 (0.00%)	0 (0.00%)	0 (0.00%)
Total	7 (100%)	6 (100%)	13 (100%)

Source: Field Study

Table 6.6: What kind of leadership do you think is good?

Statement	Name of the villages								
	Srirampoor			Chittapoor			Total		
	Women	Men	Total	Women	Men	Total	Women	Men	Total
Traditional leadership	0 (0.00%)	1 (10%)	1 (5.88%)	1 (16.67%)	2 (11.76%)	3 (13.04%)	1 (7.69%)	3 (9.04%)	4 (10%)
Party based leadership	2 (28.86%)	1 (10%)	3 (17.64%)	0 (0.00%)	6 (49.05%)	6 (26.04%)	2 (15.38%)	7 (28.22%)	9 (22.5.5%)
Leadership from women	3 (42.58%)	5 (50%)	8 (47.05%)	4 (66.66%)	3 (17.64%)	7 (30.43%)	7 (53.84%)	8 (42.33%)	15 (37.5%)
Leadership from men	1 (14.28%)	3 (30%)	4 (23.43%)	1 (16.67%)	3 (17.64%)	4 (17.39%)	2 (15.38%)	6 (20.51%)	8 (20%)
No response	1 (14.28%)	0 (0.00%)	1 (5.88%)	0 (0.00%)	3 (17.64%)	3 (13.04%)	1 (7.69%)	3 (0.00%)	4 (10%)
Total	7 (100%)	10 (100%)	17 (100%)	6 (100%)	17 (100%)	23 (100%)	13 (100%)	27 (100%)	40 (100%)

Source: Field Study

Table 6.7: As a Gram Panchayat leader, did you fulfill the basic needs of village people?

Response	Name of the villages								
	Srirampoor			Chittapoor			Total		
	Women	Men	Total	Women	Men	Total	Women	Men	Total
Yes	6 (85.71%)	9 (90%)	15 (88.23%)	6 (100%)	15 (88.23%)	21 (91.30%)	12 (92.30%)	24 (88.88%)	36 (90%)
No	1 (14.28%)	1 (10%)	2 (11.76%)	0 (0.00%)	2 (11.76%)	2 (8.70%)	1 (7.69%)	3 (11.11%)	4 (10%)
Noresponse	0 (0.00%)	0 (0.00%)	0 (0.00%)	0 (0.00%)	0 (0.00%)	0 (0.00%)	0 (0.00%)	0 (0.00%)	0 (0.00%)
Total	7 (100%)	10 (100%)	17 (100%)	6 (100%)	17 (100%)	23 (100%)	13 (100%)	27 (100%)	40 (100%)

Source: Field Study

Table 6.8: How did you get involved in Gram Panchayat politics?

Statement	Name of the villages						
	Srirampoor		Chittapoor		Total		Total
	Female	Male	Female	Male	Female	Male	
Of your own accord	3 (42.85%)	5 (50%)	2 (33.33%)	6 (35.29%)	5 (38.46%)	11 (64.70%)	16 (40%)
On persuasion by family or friend	3 (42.85%)	2 (20%)	1 (16.66%)	3 (17.64%)	4 (30.76%)	5 (18.71%)	9 (22.5%)
On the initiative of the people	0 (0.00%)	1 (100%)	1 (16.66%)	6 (35.29%)	1 (7.69%)	7 (25.92%)	8 (20%)
On being asked by a political party	1 (14.28%)	2 (20%)	2 (33.33%)	2 (11.76%)	3 (23.07%)	4 (14.81%)	7 (17.5%)
Total	7 (100%)	10 (100%)	6 (100%)	17 (100%)	13 (100%)	27 (100%)	40 (100%)

Source: Field Study

Table 6.9: Do you agree with the view that thePanchayat Raj has brought about satisfactory conditions for villagers?

Response	Name of the villages								
	Srirampoor			Chittapoor			Total		
	Women	Men	Total	Women	Men	Total	Women	Men	Total
Yes	5 (71.42%)	8 (80%)	13 (76.47%)	6 (100%)	13 (76.47%)	19 (82.68%)	11 (84.61%)	21 (77.77%)	32 (80%)
No	1 (14.28%)	0 (0.00%)	1 (5.88%)	0 (0.00%)	3 (17.64%)	3 (13.04%)	1 (7.69%)	3 (11.11%)	4 (10%)
No Response	1 (14.28%)	2 (20%)	3 (17.64%)	0 (0.00%)	1 (5.88%)	1 (4.28%)	1 (7.69%)	3 (11.11%)	4 (10%)
Total	7 (100%)	10 (100%)	17 (100%)	6 (100%)	17 (100%)	23 (100%)	13 (100%)	27 (100%)	40 (100%)

Source: Field Study

Table 6.10: Do you agree with the view that the establishment of the Panchayati Raj system has brought about satisfactory improvement in conditions for women?

Response	Name of the villages								
	Srirampoor			Chittapoor			Total		
	Women	Men	Total	Women	Men	Total	Women	Men	Total
Yes	4 (57.14%)	5 (50%)	9 (52.94%)	3 (50%)	8 (47.05%)	11 (47.82%)	7 (53.84%)	13 (48.14%)	20 (50%)
No	3 (42.84%)	2 (20%)	5 (29.41%)	2 (33.33%)	5 (29.41%)	7 (30.43%)	5 (38.46%)	7 (25.92%)	12 (30%)
No Response	0 (0.00%)	3 (30%)	3 (17.64%)	1 (16.66%)	4 (23.52%)	5 (21.73%)	1 (7.69%)	7 (25.92%)	8 (20%)
Total	7 (100%)	10 (100%)	17 (100%)	6 (100%)	17 (100%)	23 (100%)	13 (100%)	27 (100%)	40 (100%)

Source: Field Study

Table 6.11: How much progress has there been in village development work since the establishment of the Panchjayat Raj system?

Statement	Name of the villages								
	Srirampoor			Chittapoor			Total		
	Women	Men	Total	Women	Men	Total	Women	Men	Total
Much progress	5 (71.42%)	6 (60%)	11 (64.70%)	4 (66.66%)	9 (52.94%)	13 (56.52%)	9 (69.23%)	15 (55.55%)	24 (60%)
A little progress	2 (28.52%)	2 (20%)	5 (29.41%)	1 (16.66%)	2 (11.76%)	3 (13.04%)	3 (23.07%)	5 (18.51%)	8 (20%)
Doubtful progress	0 (0.00%)	1 (10%)	1 (5.88%)	0 (0.00%)	3 (17.64%)	3 (13.04%)	0 (0.00%)	4 (14.51%)	4 (10%)
No response	0 (0.00%)	0 (0.00%)	0 (0.00%)	1 (16.66%)	3 (17.64%)	4 (17.39%)	1 (7.69%)	3 (11.11%)	4 (10%)
Total	7 (100%)	10 (100%)	17 (100%)	6 (100%)	17 (100%)	23 (100%)	13 (100%)	27 (100%)	40 (100%)

Source: Field Study

Table 6.12: Do you agree with the view that the benefits of the Panchayats' development work are felt by poor people?

Response	Name of the villages								
	Srirampoor			Chittapoor			Total		
	Women	Men	Total	Women	Men	Total	Women	Men	Total
Yes	4 (57.14%)	6 (60%)	10 (58.82%)	3 (50%)	7 (41.17%)	10 (43.47%)	7 (53.84%)	13 (48.14%)	20 (50%)
No	3 (42.85%)	3 (30%)	6 (35.29%)	2 (33.33%)	7 (41.17%)	9 (39.13%)	5 (38.46%)	10 (37.03%)	15 (37.5%)
No Response	0 (0.00%)	1 (10%)	1 (5.88%)	1 (16.66%)	3 (17.64%)	4 (17.39%)	1 (7.69%)	4 (14.81%)	5 (12.5%)
Total	7 (100%)	10 (100%)	17 (100%)	6 (100%)	17 (100%)	23 (100%)	13 (100%)	27 (100%)	40 (100%)

Source: Field Study

Table 6.13: Were you a member of any political party at the time of the Panchayat elections?

Response	Name of the villages								
	Srirampoor			Chittapoor			Total		
	Women	Men	Total	Women	Men	Total	Women	Men	Total
Yes	7 (100%)	10 (100%)	17 (100%)	6 (100%)	17 (100%)	23 (100%)	13 (100%)	27 (100%)	40 (100%)
No	0 (0.00%)	0 (0.00%)	0 (0.00%)	0 (0.00%)	0 (0.00%)	0 (0.00%)	0 (0.00%)	0 (0.00%)	0 (0.00%)
No Response	0 (0.00%)	0 (0.00%)	0 (0.00%)	0 (0.00%)	0 (0.00%)	0 (0.00%)	0 (0.00%)	0 (0.00%)	0 (0.00%)
Total	7 (100%)	10 (100%)	17 (100%)	6 (100%)	17 (100%)	23 (100%)	13 (100%)	27 (100%)	40 (100%)

Source: Field Study

Table 6.13 A. IfYes;

Party wise response	Name of the villages								
	Srirampoor			Chittapoor			Total		
Party wise categories	Women	Men	Total	Women	Men	Total	Women	Men	Total
Congress	5 (71.47%)	7 (70%)	12 (70.58%)	6 (100%)	8 (47.05%)	14 (60.86%)	11 (84.63%)	15 (55.55%)	26 (65%)
T.D.P	2 (28.51%)	3 (30%)	5 (29.41%)	0 (0.00%)	3 (17.05%)	3 (13.04%)	2 (15.38%)	6 (22.22%)	8 (20%)
T.R.S	0 (0.00%)	0 (0.00%)	0 (0.00%)	0 (0.00%)	5 (29.41%)	5 (21.73%)	0 (0.00%)	5 (21.73%)	5 (12.5%)
B.J.P	0 (0.00%)	0 (0.00%)	0 (0.00%)	0 (0.00%)	1 (5.88%)	1 (4.34%)	0 (0.00%)	1 (4.34%)	1 (2.5%)
Total	7 (100%)	10 (100%)	17 (100%)	6 (100%)	17 (100%)	23 (100%)	13 (100%)	27 (100%)	40 (100%)

Source: Field Study

Table 6.14: Do you realize that the Panchayat is divided into groups?

Response	Name of the villages								
	Srirampoor			Chittapoor			Total		
	Women	Men	Total	Women	Men	Total	Women	Men	Total
Yes	7 (100%)	10 (100%)	17 (100%)	5 (88.34%)	15 (88.23%)	20 (86.95%)	12 (92.30%)	25 (92.59%)	37 (92.5%)
No	0 (0.00%)	0 (0.00%)	0 (0.00%)	0 (0.00%)	0 (0.00%)	0 (0.00%)	0 (0.00%)	0 (0.00%)	0 (0.00%)
No Response	0 (0.00%)	0 (0.00%)	0 (0.00%)	1 (16.66%)	2 (11.76%)	3 (13.04%)	1 (7.69%)	2 (7.40%)	3 (7.5%)
Total	7 (100%)	10 (100%)	17 (100%)	6 (100%)	17 (100%)	23 (100%)	13 (100%)	27 (100%)	40 (100%)

Source: Field Study

Bibliography

Austine, Granville. *The Indian Constitution: Cornerstone of a Nation.* Bombay: Oxford University Press, 1976.

Basu, Aparna and Ray, Bharati. (2nd edition), *Women's Struggle: A History of the All India Women Conference, 1927-2002.* Delhi: Manohar, 2003.

Basu, Aparna. "Role of Women in the Freedom Movement." In *Indian Women From Purdah to Modernity,* Delhi: Vikas, 1976.

Basu, Aparna. *Mridula Sarabhai: Rebel With A Cause,* Delhi: Oxford University Press, 1996.

Biju, M. R. "Women Empowerment in India, Changing Socio Political Equations." In *Women's Empowerment- Politics and Policies,* edited by M. R. Buju, 231-250. New Delhi: Mittal Publications, 2005.

Chattopadhyaya, Kamaladevi. *Indian Women's Battle for Freedom.* New Delhi: Abhinav Publications, 1983.

Desai, Vasant. *Panchayati Raj: power to the people.* Bombay: Himalaya Publishing House, 1990.

Dey, S.K. *Panchayati Raj in India.* Bombay: Asia Publishing House, 1961.

Forbes, Geraldine. *Women in Modern India.* Cambridge: Cambridge University Press, 1998.

Gangrade, K.D. *Emerging Pattern of Leadership.* Delhi: Rachana Publications, 1974.

Jain, L. C. *Grass without Roots.* New Delhi: Sage Publishers, 1984.

Jain, S. P and Thomas W. Hochegesang (Eds.). *Emerging Trends in Panchayati Raj (Rural Local Self Government) in India.* Hyderabad: NIRD, 1995.

Jain, S. P. *Devolution of Power, Functions and Authority to Panchayats in Different States.* Hyderabad: National Institute of Rural Development, 1999.

Jain, S.P. Naidu, N.Y. *Panchayati Raj and Social change: A Study in Assam.* Hyderabad: National Institute of Rural Development, 1995.

Joshi, H.G. *Dynamics of Women Leadership.* New Delhi: Ace Books India, 2010.

Kashyap, Anibban. *Panchayati Raj: Views of the Founding Fathers and Recommendations of Different Committees.* New Delhi: Concers Books, 1989.

Kashyap, Anirban. *Panchayat Raj: Views of the Founding Fathers and Recommendations of Different Committees.* New Delhi: Lancers Books, 1989.

Kaur, Manmohan. *Role of Women in the Freedom Movement, 1857-1947.* New Delhi: Sterling, 1968.

Kerala Institute of Local Administration. *Hand Book on Transfer of Functions and Schemes to Local Self Government Institutions.* Trissur: KILA, 1997.

Klenke, Karin. *Women and Leadership – A Contextual Perspective.* New York: Springer Publishing Company, 1996.

Kothari, Rajni. *Caste in Indian Politics.* New Delhi: Orient Longman, 1970.

Lerner, Gerda. *The Majority Finds Its Past, Placing Women in History.* London: Oxford University Press, 1981.

Madan, N.L. *Indian Political System: Socio-Economic Dimensions.* Delhi: Ajantha Publishers, 1989.

Maddick, Henry. *Democracy, Decentralization and Development.* Bombay: Asia Publishing House, 1963.

Maddick, Henry. *Panchayat Raj: A Study of Rural Local Government in India.* London: Longrnan Group Ltd., 1970.

Mandal, Jyotirmay. *Women and Reservation in India.* Delhi: Kalpz Publications, 2003.

Manikyamba, P. *Women in Panchayati Structures.* New Delhi: Gain Publishing House, 1989.

Mathew, George. (Ed.). *Panchayati Raj: From Legislation to Movement.* New Delhi: Concept, 1994.

Mathew, George. *Status of Panchayati Raj in the States and Union Territories of India.* New Delhi: Concept Publishing Company, 2000.

Mathur, Om Prakash. *Decentralisation in India: A Report Card.* New Delhi: National Institute of Public Finance and Policy, 1999

Mathur, P. C. *Political Dynamics of Panchayati Raj.* New Delhi: Konark Publications, 1991.

Meenakshisundaram, S.S. "Decentralization in Developing Countries." In *Decentralization and Local Politics: Reading in India Government and Politics,* edited by S.N. Jha and P.C. Mathur, 54-69, London: Sage Publications, 1999.

Mehta, S.R. *Emerging Pattern of Rural Leadership.* New Delhi: Wiely Eastern Private Limited, 1972.

Menon, Nivedita. *Gender and Politics in India.* New Delhi: National Publishing House, 1995.

Mishra, Anil Dutt. *Panchayati Raj: (Gandhian perspective).* New Delhi:Mittal Publications, 2002.

Mishra, S.N. Lokesh Kumar, Chaitali Pal. *New Panchayati Raj in Action.* New Delhi: Mittal Publications, 1996.

Nagendra, Ambedkar S. *New Panchayati Raj at Work.* Jaipur: Add Publications, 2000.

Nandal, Roshi. *Women Development and Panchayati Raj*. New Delhi: Mittal Publications, 1996.

Narayana, Lakshmi H.D. *Democracy in Rural India*. Delhi: National Publishing House, 1980.

Palanithurai, G. *Capacity Building for Local Body Leaders*. New Delhi: Concept Publishing Company, 2001.

Palaniturai, G, and others. *Major Issue in Panchayati Raj System*. New Delhi: Publishers Distributors, 1997.

Pattanaik, S.N. *Rural Women Panchayati Raj and Development*. New Delhi: Arise Publishers, 2010.

Paxton, P. Melanic M.Hughes. *Women, Politics and Power – A Global Perspective*. Loss Angels: Pine Forge Press, 2007.

Rahul, Mudgal. *Local Self Government in India*. Jaipur: Book Enclave, 1998.

Raj, Singh. *Panchayati Raj Manual: A Socio-Historical- Legal Perspective*. New Delhi: Anmol Publications, 1996.

Ranga Rao, S.P. *Panchayati Raj and the Constitution (Background Paper)*. Hyderabad: Prakasam Institute of Development Studies, 1989.

Reddy, M. Gopinath and Madhusudan Bandi. "The Status of Panchayati Raj Institutions (PRIs) in Andhra Pradesh and Karnataka: A Comparison". In *Dynamics of Grassroots Governance in India: Dreams and Realities* (Vol. 1 of 2), edited by D. Sunder Ram, 152-173. New Delh: Kanishka Publishers, 2007.

Sapru, R.K. *Public Policy: Art and Craft of Policy Analysis*. New Delhi: PHI Learing Private Limited, 2010.

Shah, B.L. *Panchayati Raj- The Role of Panchayati Raj in Independent Rural Development*. New Delhi: Cosmo Publications, 1980.

Sharma, K.M. *All India Panchayat Digest*. New Delhi: Kamal Publishers, 1995.

Sharma, Kailashchandra. *Leadership in Panchayati Raj*. Jaipur: Print Well Publishers, 1996.

Sharma, S.R. *Panchayati Raj and Education in India (Panchayats in free India)*. New Delhi: Mittal Publishers, 1994.

Shivaiah, M. *Panchayati Raj: A Policy Perspective*. Hyderabad:National Institute of Rural Development, 1986.

Singh, J.L. Pandy, G.P. *50 Years of Panchayati Raj and Rural Development*. Delhi: Manak Publications, 1998.

Singh, K.K. Ali, A. *Role of Panchayati Raj Institutions for Rural Development*. New Delhi: Sarup and Sons Publications, 2001.

Singh, S.S. Suresh Mishra and Sanjay Pratap. *Legislative Status of panchjayati Raj in India*. New Delhi: Institute of Public Administration, 1997.

Verma, S.L. *Panchayati Raj Gram Swaraj and Federal Polity:Decentralization and Political Development in India.* Jaipur: Rawat Pblications, 1990.

Vohra, A.L. Vashist, S.R. *Panchayati Raj and Education (vol.I):Panchayati Raj in Post Independence India.* New Delhi: Akash Deep Publishing House, 1998.

Zaid, Ijlal, Anis S.M. *Politics, Power and Leadership in Rural India.* New Delhi: Common Wealth Publishers, 1988.

Journals/Articles

Basu, Aparna. "Women's Struggle for the Vote." *Indian Historical Review,* 35, No.1, (2008): N.A.

Beteille, Adre. "Empowerment." *Economic and Political Weekly,* 6-13, 1999: 589-597.

Biju, M.R. "Women Empowerment in India: Changing Socio-Political Equations." *South Asian Journal of Socio-Political Studies,* vol.6, No.1, (2005): 45-49.

Bohra, O.P. "Women in Decentralized Democracy." *Journal of Rural Development,* Vol.16 (4), (1994): N.A.

Datta, Prabhat and Panchali Bhattacharya Sen. "Participatory rural governance in India." *The Indian Journal of Public Administration,* Vol. XLVI, (2000): 38-49.

Deepti, Agarwal. "Empowerment of Rural women in India." *Social Welfare,* Vol. 48, (2001): 11-36.

Devasia, Leelamma. "Rural women's Empowerment: A Grassroot level Experiment." *Social Welfare,* Vol. 48, (2001): 5-10.

Dubeshi, P.R. "Decentralization and Rural development." *Kurukshetra,* Vol. 29, (1990):N.A.

The Economic Weekly (Special Correspondent). "Panchayat Raj in Andhra Pradesh." *The Economic Weekly,* (1960): 1681-1682.

Ghosh, Anjana. "Women Reservation: A Reflection on Women Empowerment." *Journal of Indian Anthropological Society,* No.37, (2002): 253-240.

Ghosh, Dilip. "Grassroots women leaders: Who are they? A Study in a West Bengal District." *Journal of Rural Development,* Vol. 16 (2), (1997): N.A.

Gurumoorthy, T.R. "Self Help Groups Empower Rural Women." *Kuruksherta,* Vol. 48, (2000): 36-39.

Jain, L.C "Panchayats- remove the weeds." *Kurukshetra,* Vol. XLIV, No. 7, (1996): 6-8.

Jain, S.P. "The Gram Sabha: Gateway to Grass Roots Democracy." *Journal of Rural Development*, Vo. 16, (1997): 557 – 573.

Jayant, P. "Democratic decentralization: A Revival of Gandhiji vision." *Kurukshetra*, Vol. XLIII, (1994): 18-.

Kannabiran, Kalpana, Vasanth Kannabiran and Volga. "Andhra Pradesh - Women's Rights and Naxalite Groups." *Economic and Political Weekly*, 39 (45), (2004): 4874-4877.

Kaul, Shashi and Shradha Sahni. "Participation of Women in Panchayati Raj Institution", *Studies on Home and Community Science*, 3(1), (2009): 29-38.

Majoj, Pant. "Women Empowerment – Perspective and Approach." *The Administrator*, Vol.45, No.2, (2002): 73-77.

Malavika, Karlekar. "Focus on Women's Empowerment." *Indian Journal of Gender Studies*, Vol.11, No.2, 2004: 145-155.

Mishra, Shweta "Women and 73rd Constitutional Amendment Act: A Critical Appraisal." *Social Action, Indian social Institute*, Vol. 47, (1997): N.A.

Panda, Snehalata. "Emerging Pattern of Leadership among Rural Women in Orissa." *Indian Journal of Public Administration*, Vol. 42, (1996): 3-4.

Parida, Dayanidhi. "Women and Panchayat Raj – A Study." Orissa Review, February – March, (2010): 22-23.

Rao, Vasudeva, D. "Emerging Leadership of women in institutions of Local Governance: A Study in Andhra Pradesh." *Social Action, Institute of Social Action*, Vol. 53, (2003): N.A.

Singh, Hoshiar "Decentralization thro': Constitution (73rd Amendment) Act." *Kurukshetra*, New Delhi, Vol. XLI, (1993): N.A.

Singh, S.P. "Gram Panchayats: Assessing Developmental Goals, Motivational Factors and Orientation Evidence from a Study." *Journal of Rural Development*, NIRD, Hyderabad, Vol. 19, (2000): N.A.

Spio, K. "The Role of women in the rural society." *Journal of Rural Development*, New Delhi, Vol. 16(3), (1997): N.A.

Documents

Documentation on Panchayati Raj: Summaries of Major Reports, Centre for Panchayati Raj, NIRD, Hyderabad, 1991.

India, Panchayati Report 2001: Four Decades of Decentralized Governance in Rural India, NIRD, Volume-II, 2001.

Andhra Pradesh Panchayati Raj (Reservation of seats of ward members and offices of sarpanches of Gram Panchayats) Rules,1995, G.O.MS.NO. 285, Panchayati Raj and Rural Development (Elec-III) Department, dt.20.5.1995.

District's Documents of Zilla Panchayati Raj Office, Nizamabad, 2003.

Janabha-25-06-2001, Gram Pancahayat Office-Srirampoor, Mandal: Balkonda, District: Nizamabad, A.P.

Janabha-2001, Gram Panchahayat Office- Chittapoor, Mandal: Balkonda, District: Nizamabad, A.P.

Internet Articles

Coonrod, John and Banavalikar, Supriya. "The women and Panchayati Raj campaign" http://www.thp.org/india/trip803.

University of Georgia. "Points of Pride" University of Georgia, http://www.uga.edu/profile/pride.html.

Devi, Jagrani. "Women leadership in Panchayati Raj" http://www.pucl.org/topics/gender/2003/panchayats.htm.

Government of Andhra Pradesh. "Nizamabad District Profile" http://nizamabad.nic.in/code/ profile.

Inter-Parliamentary Union, "Participation of Women in Political Life - An assessment of developments in national parliaments, political parties, governments and the Inter-Parliamentary Union, five years after the Fourth World Conference on Women, Geneva" http://www.ipu.org/PDF/publications/womenplus5 en.pdf.

Mohanty, Bidyut. "Women's Presence in Panchayats (Village Councils) in India: A New Challenge to Patriarchy" http://www.undp.org/dpa/choices/2000/march/pg20.htm.

Ruth J. Alsop, Anirudh Krishna and Disa Sjoblom. "Inclusion and Local Elected Governments: The Panchayat raj System in India" www.*siteresources.worldbank.org.*

Smitha, K C. "Socio-economic Determinants of Women leadership At the grass-roots Institute for social and economic change" www.isec.ac.in/CPIGD-WorkingPapers.pdf.

Index

About Author

Sunkari Satyam is now with Council for Social Development, from Political Science discipline and specialized in Public Policy. He received his Ph.D. from University of Hyderabad. He has been engaging in social science researches such as Analytical, Participatory, Action, Evaluation and Monitoring. His publications primarily focus on Rural Poverty, Social Justice, Welfare and Developmental Policies of Scheduled Castes and Scheduled Tribes, and Women in Panchayati Raj Institutions. The present book helps to policy makers, developmental practitioners, social sciences' research scholars and NGOs to understand women in grass-root politics and their hurdles in contemporary political spheres.